AF323699

OPTIONS TRADING FOR BEGINNERS

Ready-to-use beginner's guide to gaining the confidence needed to start investing, making money and creating an alternative passive income with proven strategies

Nick Tudor

TABLE OF CONTENTS

Introduction

An option is an agreement on the underlying shares of stock. It is an agreement to exchange shares at a fixed price over a specific time frame (they can be bought or sold). The first thing that you should understand about options is the following. Why would someone get involved with the options trading in the first place? Most people come to options trading with the hope of earning profits from trading the options themselves. And that is probably going to describe most readers. But to truly understand what you are doing, you need to understand why options exist, to begin with.

There are probably three main reasons that options on stocks exist. The first reason is that it allows people that have shares of stock to earn money from their investment in the form of regular income. So, it can be an alternative to dividend income or even enhance dividend income. As we are going to see you, if you own a minimum of 100 shares of some stock, this is a possibility. Then you can sell options against the stock and earn income from that over time intervals lasting from a week to a month, generally speaking. Such a move entails some risk, but people will enter positions of that type when the relative risk is low.

The second reason that people get involved with options is that they offer insurance against a collapse of the stock. So, once again, an option involves being able to trade shares of the stock at a fixed price that is set at the time the contract is originated. One type of contract allows the buyer to purchase shares, the other allows the buyer to sell shares. This allows people who own large numbers of shares to purchase something that provides protection of their investment that would allow them to sell the shares at a fixed price, if their stock was declining by vast amounts on the market. So, the concept is exactly like paying insurance premiums. It is unclear how many people use this in practice, but this is one of the reasons that options exist. The way this would work would be that you pay someone a premium to secure the right to sell them your stock at a fixed price over some time frame. Then if the share price drops well below that degree to price, you would still be able to sell your shares and avoid huge losses that were occurring on the market.

The third reason that I would give for the existence of options is that it provides a way for people to decide to purchase shares of stock at the prices that they find attractive, which are not necessarily available on the market. So, there is a degree of speculation here. But let us just say that a particular stock you are interested in is trading at $100 a share. Furthermore, let us assume that people are incredibly bullish on the stock and they are expecting it to rise by a great deal in the coming weeks. Maybe, it is earnings season.

During earnings season, stock can move by massive amounts. But before the earnings call, nobody knows whether the stock is going to go up or down or by how much it is going to move. An options contract could allow someone to speculate and set up a situation where they could profit from a huge move upward without having actually to invest in the stock.

So in that situation, if the stock declined instead, they would not be out of much money. Just for an example, let us say they buy an options contract that allows them to purchase the shares (of the stock currently at $100) for $102, and the option costs two dollars per share. So, the stock would have to go to $104 or higher to make it worth it.

Typically, options contracts involve 100 shares. So, if the speculator bets wrong, the most they would be out would be $200.

Let us just say, after the earnings call, the share price jumps to $120. The speculator can exercise the option, which means they buy the shares at $102 per share. Then they can sell the stock on the market at the price of $120 per share. Considering the investment to buy the options contract, that leaves them with the sixteen 16 dollars per-share profit. Now, you might say well why didn't they just buy the shares that $100 a share? The reason is if they did that, they would be exposed to the stock to the fullest extent possible. Like we said, earnings calls can go both ways. Just recently, Netflix announced that they lost subscribers. In after-hours trading alone, the stock lost $43 per share. So, in our little example, we could say that the stock dropped instead of gaining, let us say to $80 per share. In that case, our speculator would have been in a significant point of pain had they purchase the shares ahead of time. By doing the option instead, they set themselves up for profit while only risking a $200 loss. And it turns out that there are strategies you can use with options to profit no matter which way the stock moves. So, I did not want to get too far ahead of we, but an experienced options trader would have set up a trade designed to earn profits either way.

1.   What Does It Trade

Futures contracts include nearly all the commodities that are used by individuals in their routine lives and also the chief investment areas, and these are traded at exchanges throughout the world.

There are various categories of futures markets, for example, metals, grains, energies, interest rates, stock indexes, currencies, and so on. One can choose the particular commodities, contract sizes and periods for trading.

Many essential factors need to be taken into account before one starts trading.

Margins:

Before you start taking part in trading activities, you will have to pay a margin to the exchanges as your insurance that the contract conditions will be fulfilled. There can be significant differences in the size of margins for different commodity contracts. For instance, the margin for an index contract, such as the S&P 500 can be quite high ($25,000), while that of the grain contracts can be quite low ($400). The size of the contract and the instability of the commodity determine the margin. You should make sure that you have sufficient cash in your trading account that can cover your margin. If profits are made on your contract position, you will get your margin back, in addition to the profit. However, if it is making a loss and the loss amount is more significant than what is available in your trading account, your broker will call you and ask you to add more funds to your account as soon as possible to sustain your position. This is known as a margin call.

Volume:

The volume of the contract should be checked before you become involved in a trade. Volume refers to the number of contracts that are traded every day. The volume for a given day can be determined by adding just the amount of lengthy contracts for a day, while leaving out the short contracts. The future market is known as a net sum zero game, which means that for each winning trade, you have a losing trade, and for every trade, there is someone who is buying and someone who is selling a contract. Those markets that have high volume offer you the opportunity to enter and leave a trade at your desired levels. However, when there is minimal volume, there may be no party on the other side to take your trade. This indicates that there are chances that your orders will be poorly executed.

Open Interest:

This refers to the number of contracts that are still open at the closing of each day. It also serves as an excellent example of the liquidity of the market. When open interest is low, there is low trading interest and there is high possibility of bad "fills".

Volatility:

When a specific commodity has a highly volatile price, which quickly shifts across an extensive range each day, it may be possible that your trading account gets empty rapidly, even if you have made the right predictions about the long-run trend. You must examine the volatility of a commodity in the past before deciding to trade so that you can determine if the volatility is appropriate for your risk profile. There may be high open interest and volume of certain commodities; however, it may be implied that you should restrict your trade to other commodities that exhibit low volatility. This means that you should carry out trade of commodities whose normal trading range is narrow.

If you are an experienced trader and you want to take a chance at taking on the market, you probably know what you want in a brokerage like comprehensive trading platforms, innovative strategy tools, premium research, and low costs. We have chosen some of the best brokers that you can use only in several different categories, so you will be able to choose one that is based on your priorities.

These following brokers have great pricing over their competitors and they have great trading tools and platforms:

Interactive Brokers and Options House have a powerful combination that each trader wants: Advanced trading tools and platforms paired with low commissions. Interactive Brokers tend to be the choice of traders that like per share pricing and can meet a minimum account of $10,000 with a minimum monthly commission of $10. This slightly affects their rating. Options House, on the other hand, gives traders a flat rate, and they don't require a minimum balance. The downside is they don't have forex trading. Interactive Brokers gives you access to forex, futures, and precious metals.

These brokers offer the most powerful platforms that are available without any fees or minimums:

Options House and Interactive Brokers have robust platforms. Charles Schwab and TD Ameritrade also surpass others. TD Ameritrade probably has the best platform out there, thinkorswim, as well as Trade Architect that is very simple to use. Charles Schwab also gives you two great platforms: Streetsamrt.com is an excellent platform for beginners. StreetSmart Edge is a more advanced functionality in charting.

Both of which can be used by traders and they don't require any balance or activity minimums. Remember that there is an avoidable account minimum account balance of $1,000.

These brokers offer potent tools and competitive pricing for options traders:

TradeStation and OptionsXpress are two more great options for traders to use. Which one you like the best will depend on what you are looking for in trade activity and platform needs. TradeStation is aimed more towards the professional trader. This platform will cost $99.95 each month, which is waived if you trade at least 5,000 shares, ten futures options or round-turn futures contracts, 50 options contracts, or carried a $100,000 balance. TradeStation's pricing is favorable to bulk traders, which give per-contract, flat fees, or volume discounts. OptionsXpress don't require trade or account balance minimums, carry the extra fees, or offers competitive commissions, and they don't have vigorous trading. Trades with OptionsXpress only cost $1.25 for each contract for active traders, and they have a $12.95 minimum charge for ten or fewer contracts

Traders that utilize margin needs to prioritize broker's margin rates while they search. These online brokers have the lowest margin rates:

None of the others can even come close to Interactive Brokers when you look at their margin rates. If margin rates are your priority, then this is a good option for you. This broker will charge you a grouped rate that is based on the balance of your account but also has a calculator to help traders to perform their math quicker. Interactive Brokers do have a minimum of monthly trade. EOption's deposit requirement is a lot lower, and they have a more reasonable trade requirement. They only charge a $50 inactivity fee when you don't trade at least two times a year or who has less than $100,000 in debit or credit balances. Both of these options have competitive commissions for their options and stock trades.

The first thing you should do before jumping on board and starting to trade options is to figure out what your end goal is. Every trader should have a plan and stick to that plan, even when it seems like it is stalling. If you don't have a plan then you are just going to be haphazardly trading all over the place with no rhyme or reason. And even worse – you are going to be letting emotion get in the way of your trading.

Trust me, when it comes to options emotions get involved. Depending on what the market is doing, you might see your options melting right before your eyes. When that happens, emotions are going to come up in a big way and that can lead to bad decisions.

Of course, before that happens you need to mitigate your risks as much as possible. But it's not possible to account for everything, and sometimes things are just going to go south. The first thing you need to do is have a clear understanding of how options work. If you don't understand expiration dates, the Greeks, the differences between calls and puts, you need to study those things right now. You need to know them before you jump off into different options strategies.

2.   How The Market Works

It is essential to focus on the fact that options expire. Time works against an option: the less time on the contract, the lower the probability that market prices will move in the options' favor. This characteristic of options is known as time decay.

If a call option reaches the expiration date and its strike price is below the market price, it could be exercised, which means the owner of the option could buy the 100 shares of stock. This has two advantages. The stock could be immediately sold at the higher market price, earning the investor a profit. Alternatively, if they wanted to own the stock, the option gave them the ability to get the shares at a discounted price.

If the strike price is above the market price at that point, the option is worthless, because there would be no point in buying shares of stock at a higher price. In the industry, they say the option expires worthless.

For a put option, on the date of expiration, it's considered valuable if the strike price is above the market price. In that case, the investor can exercise the option by selling the shares of stock at a price that is higher than the market price, earning a profit.

Put options can also be used in an alternative way. Some investors that hold a large number of shares may buy put options as a form of insurance. This can protect them from a catastrophic loss if the stock undergoes a significant decline in price. A put option provides a safety valve they can use to protect their shares.

If the strike price of a put option is below the market price, it expires worthless. An investor is not going to opt to sell shares when they would sell for less than market price.

Basic of contracts and terminology

An options contract sounds fancy but it's a pretty simple concept.

- It's a contract. That means it's a legal agreement between a buyer and a seller.

- It allows the purchaser of the contract to purchase or dispose of an asset with a fixed amount.

- The purchase is optional – so the buyer of the contract does not have to buy or sell the asset.

- The contract has an expiration date, so the purchaser – if they choose to exercise their right – must make the trade on or before the expiration date.

- The purchaser of the contract pays a non-refundable fee for the contract.

While the focus of this manuscript is on options contracts related to the stock market, some options contracts take place in all aspects of daily life including real estate and speculation. A simple example illustrates the concept of an options contract.

Suppose you are itching to buy a BMW and you've decided the model you want must be silver. You drop by a local dealer and it turns out they don't have a silver model in stock. The dealer claims he can get you one by the end of the month. You say you'll take the car if the dealer can get it by the last day of the month and he'll sell it to you for $67,500. He agrees and requires you to put a $3,000 deposit on the car.

If the last day of the month arrives and the dealer hasn't produced the car, then you're freed from the contract and get your money back. In the event he does produce the car at any date before the end of the month, you have the option to buy it or not. If you wanted the car you can buy it, but of course, you can't be forced to buy the car, and maybe you've changed your mind in the interim.

The right is there but not the obligation to purchase, in short, no pressure if you decided not to push through with the purchase of the car. If you decide to let the opportunity pass, however, since the dealer met his end of the bargain and produced the car, you lose the $3,000 deposit.

In this case, the dealer, who plays the role of the writer of the contract, has the obligation to follow through with the sale based upon the agreed upon price.

Suppose that when the car arrives at the dealership, BMW announces it will no longer make silver cars. As a result, prices of new silver BMWs that were the last ones to roll off the assembly line, skyrocket. Other dealers are selling their silver BMWs for $100,000. However, since this dealer entered into an options contract with you, he must sell the car to you for the pre-agreed price of $67,500. You decide to get the car and drive away smiling, knowing that you saved $32,500 and that you could sell it at a profit if you wanted to.

The situation here is capturing the essence of options contracts, even if you've never thought of haggling with a car dealer in those terms.

An option is in a sense a kind of bet. In the example of the car, the bet is that the dealer can produce the exact car you want within the specified period and at the agreed upon price. The dealer is betting too. He bets that the pre-agreed to price is a good one for him. Of course, if BMW stops making silver cars, then he's made the wrong bet.

It can work the other way too. Let's say that instead of BMW deciding not to make silver cars anymore when your car is being driven onto the lot, another car crashes into it. Now your silver BMW has a small dent on the rear bumper with some scratches. As a result, the car has immediately declined in value. But if you want the car, since you've agreed to the options contract, you must pay $67,500, even though with the dent it's only really worth $55,000. You can walk away and lose your $3,000 or pay what is now a premium price on a damaged car.

Another example that is commonly used to explain options contracts is the purchase of a home to be built by a developer under the agreement that certain conditions are met. The buyer will be required to put a non-refundable down payment or deposit on the home. Let's say that the developer agrees to build them the home for $300,000 provided that a new school is built within 5 miles of the development within one year. So, the contract expires within a year. At any time during the year, the buyer has the option to go forward with the construction of the home for $300,000 if the school is built. The developer has agreed to the price no matter what. So if the housing market in general and the construction of the school, in particular, drive up demand for housing in the area, and the developer is selling new homes that are now priced at $500,000, he has to sell this home for $300,000 because that was the price agreed to when the contract was signed. The home buyer got what they wanted, being within 5 miles of the new school with the home price fixed at $300,000.

Basic terminology

It is advisable to learn as much as possible about options pricing especially at the primary level. Below is some of the most basic terminology that pertains to options pricing.

At-the-money options: These are options contracts with a strike price that is the same as that of the market price of the underlying commodity.

Contract: This is an option that consists of 100 shares of a specified underlying security.

Covered Put: This is an options contract where the option writer has a short position within the underlying security based on a share-for-share basis.

Covered Call: In this instance, the option contract writer has a long position on the underlying security based on a share-for-share term.

Covered Writer - This term refers to an options seller who also owns the underlying security. The owner hedges the security against the option.

Date: This is the date when an option contract expires and becomes null and void. A lot of options contracts expire on the third Friday at 4.00 pm on expiration month.

Derivative: This is a security that derives its value from another security referred to as underlying security. Options contracts are a type of derivative because they derive their value from an underlying security.

Early Exercise – When you decide to exercise an options contract before it attains its expiry date. This can happen with American style options.

European Options: This term refers to a specific type of options contract which can only be exercised at a particular time just before it expires.

Holder: A trader who purchases an options contract then pays the writer a premium.

LEAPS: Long-Term Equity Anticipation Securities – these are options contracts that are publicly traded with expiration dates that extend beyond a year.

In-the-money: We say that a call option is in-the-money when the value of the underlying security is higher than the options' strike price.

Listed Option: This is a call or put option that is available for trade at the options exchange. Some of the terms about the option are determined and standardized by the exchange.

Open Interest: The sum of all outstanding options at the options market on a specific day.

Naked Option: This refers to an option's position that does not include the writer's offsetting position with the underlying security. This means that there is no protection in case the price moves in the opposite direction.

Option: An option is a financial instrument and a derivative. This derivative grants its buyer the right to an asset or security without any obligation to sell or buy. However, this is usually for a specified period and at a set price.

Out-of-the-money: An option that has no intrinsic value and that will expire worthless at the close of the trading day. For call options, this is the case when the strike price exceeds the underlying security's market price. For the put option, this is when the strike price is below the market rate of the underlying security.

Over-the-counter: This term refers to options contracts that are not traded at an exchange like other options. Such an option lacks standardized expiration dates and strike prices.

Premium: This is the overall cost of an options contract. When you buy an option, you pay an amount known as the premium. This amount combines the time value of the option and its intrinsic value.

Put: This refers to an option contract that awards a buyer the right to sell underlying security without the obligation of doing so. This right is pegged within a specific time frame and an agreed price.

Strike Price: this is the price that is agreed upon between parties at which you can exercise your options contract. For a call option, the strike is generally the price at which you can buy the contract. For put options, it refers to the price at which you can sell the option. Sometimes this price is known as the exercise price.

Terms: An options contract has conditions. These include an expiration date, strike price, underlying security and so on. These are collectively known as terms.

Writer: This is an investor who writes and sells options contracts and collects a premium as payment for the effort. As a writer, you are obligated to sell or buy the underlying security should the holder decide to exercise the option.

Underlying Security: This term refers to financial security that will be sold or bought should an option be exercised.

3. Factors Determinate Options Prices

The only way to determine the price value if an option is to establish what contributes to its value. Things are priced differently depending on their value. When you intend to purchase a car, you have probably thought of the model you intend to get. What makes a Lamborghini more expensive than a Toyota? Well, the price narrows down to the quality of the car. This applies to almost every other commodity that can be sold. The quality is usually the core determining factor while coming up with the price. When it comes to investing, the price value will discover the income you are likely to generate. If you aspire to trade in a successful venture, you may be required to use a large portion of your income equally. This is because the high quality of goods and services are highly-priced. The vice versa is also applicable. The low-priced commodities that low quality and are likely to result in a small income-generating investment. The prices will tell you a lot about the investment you choose to undertake. Below are the key influencing factors while pricing options.

The type of Options

We have two types of options: a call option, and a put option. This is the basis in establishing the price of an item. Depending on the fact the type of option involved, the costs will differ. In a call option, the investor earns the right to purchase the underlying asset at an agreed-upon duration at the set price. In a put option, the investor has the right to trade the underlying instrument at a set price within the specified period. In a situation whereby you have the long a call or are short a put, the value of the option goes high as the market value increases. When you are short a call or long a put, the option value will increase as the market value declines.

Stock Price

This is the value of a stock. In some situations, the call option may permit you to purchase a stock at an agreed-upon price. The cost of the capital may rise in the future, resulting in the option being worth more than it already is. The same applies if the prices lack the potential to increase, this will mean that the value of the stock will go low, and as a result, you encounter a loss. For instance, you may buy the stock at $ 200 and maybe shortly it has the potential of rising to $ 220.another person may obtain a share at $ 100. Soon, the value of the stock decreases to $ 70. You will end up with a loss of $ 30. Ideally, one would instead go with the capital that has the probability of increasing in the future. This way, you will end up making a profit as opposed to ending up with a loss in your investment.

Strike Price

The strike price operates the same as the stock price. A strike price refers to the fixed amount of money in which a derivative contract can be exercised or bought. While dealing with stocks, this is a term that you will come across severally. In a put option, the strike price refers to the amount that the underlying asset is traded by the option buyer while at the expiry date. In a call option, the strike price refers to the price the underlying asset can be purchased by the option buyer up to the expiry. The rates will differ depending on the type of strike price.

The Expiration Date

You have heard of some contracts being regarded as worthless upon getting to the expiry date. The reason behind it is since their value is no longer in existence once the contract expires. The expiration date in options trading refers to the duration in which an option contract is of importance and after which it is considered valueless. You find that the expiry date dramatically influences the option prices, and if you are not keen, you may end up making a loss.

This means that the best time to buy or sell options when the cost is high, that is any period before the expiry date is. You find that beginners are at times deceived and sold for an option that is almost becoming worthless and as a result, end up making losses.

Interest Rates

The interest rates do not have a massive impact on the option value, but they have minimal influence. The amount of a call option rises when there is an increase in interest rates, and the value of the put option falls. Alternatively, when the interest rates decline the value of the call option will also become lower, and the put options will rise. The second option becomes attractive when the interest rates increase. In a situation where the interest goes up, you will be able to earn more. This shows how interest rates influence prices.

Volatility

In determining the option prices, we use forward volatility. Forward volatility refers to the quantity of implied volatility during the duration in the future. The implied volatility refers to the implied movement of stocks. It acts as an indicator of the direction the stock moves. Some moves result from increases in the value of the capital. Also, some moves result from declining in the amount of money. When the stock value lowers its prices also decrease. In an event, the stock value increases the prices are also bound to increase. This is how the volatility influences the rates.

Dividends

A dividend refers to the regular total payment made by a company to its shareholders. It results from the profits made by a company. In most cases, options do not get dividends. If bonuses are given out, the option value will fluctuate. An ex-dividend date is provided once a company gives out profits. Dividends can be given out if you have stocks at the time of their release. When this occurs, it also influences the value of the capital, causing it to decrease with the number of dividends. The call value lowers, and the put value goes above in a situation whereby the bonuses increase. This is how profits influence the prices of options.

4. Buying Vs Selling

When you have options, you can do four things with them, and they are:

- Sell puts

- Buy puts

- Sell calls

- Buy calls

Purchasing stock offers you an extended position. Purchasing the call option offers you a prospective long position in that particular stock.

When you short sell a stock, you are given a short position. When you sell a naked call, you are given a prospective short position in that stock.

When you decide to purchase a put option, you are given a prospective short position in that stock.

When you sell a naked put, you are given a prospective long position in that stock. It is essential to understand these situations.

Those that purchase options are christened holders. As for the sellers of options, they are christened writers of options.

Below are the differences between the buyers and sellers.

As for the buyers- put holders and call holders- they can decide to buy or not. They have the rights to do so.

What this does is to restrict the risk of buyers of options to solely the premium that has been spent.

The sellers- put writers and call writers- are those that are under obligations to sell the option before the contract expires. What this means is that you must fulfill the promise.

It means that options sellers face a lot of risks, compared to the buyers.

It means that writers can end up losing a lot more than the options premium's value.

Why Use Options

Options are used for a lot of things;

Speculation

Speculation is that wager on where the future price of a financial instrument is going. Someone that is involved in speculation is a speculator. A speculator may feel that the price would increase because the facts state this, especially on technical analysis or fundamental analysis. A speculator is known to buy either the stock or the call option.

Using a call option to speculate, instead of purchasing the stock itself is lucrative to a lot of traders because options offer leverage.

Going for an out-of-the-money call option might end up costing few cents or dollars on the total price of a $100 stock.

Hedging

Options were created for hedging. When you hedge with options, you are clamping down on the risk at an affordable price. Many people see options as an insurance policy in the financial market, and they aren't wrong.

The way you insure your house or car is the same way that options act as insurance for the investments you intend to buy, for when downtime come. Let's say you want to purchase technology stocks, but you want to reduce the losses that you face. By making use of put options, you can restrict the downside risk, while benefiting from the upside.

When you make use of call options, you tend to reduce your risks.

Buying Calls

Buying calls is a more advanced form of training than selling covered calls. But it's not that complicated, so let's dive in.

What you're actually buying

Remember that one option contract is for 100 shares, so you'll need to be able to buy 100 shares of the stock in order to exercise your right to buy.

Also, remember that an options contract has a deadline. If the stock price falls to exceed the strike price by the deadline, you're out of luck and will lose whatever money that you invested in the premium. In relative terms, the premium price will be small, so chances are if you are careful and not starting out by buying large numbers of options contracts, you won't be out that much money.

Your goal buying options contracts

The goal when purchasing options contracts is to buy a stock at a price that is lower than its current market value. In other words, you want the stock price to be significantly higher than the strike price so that you're enjoying significant savings in purchasing the stock. When evaluating your options, you'll need to take into account the added costs of the premium paid plus commissions. In some cases, commissions can be substantial, so make sure you know what they are ahead of time so that you choose an excellent strike price and exercise your options at the right time.

You're a trader, not an investor

You may be mentally conditioned to think in terms of investing. An investor wants to build a diversified portfolio over a long time period that they believe will increase in value over the long term. A trader operates in the same universe but has different goals. You are after short term profits – not investments. You are not going to hold this stock. If you were interested in holding the stock, you would simply buy it at the lower price that is currently on offer. Your goal is to be able to buy at the strike price when the stock has increased significantly in price and then sell it immediately so that you can pocket the profits.

Let's take an example. Suppose that XYZ corporation is currently selling at $30 a share. People are expecting the stock to rise, and some people are really bullish about their short-term prospects. If you are an investor, your goal is to get the stock at the lowest possible price and then hold it long term. If you are using strategies like dollar-cost averaging, you might be buying a few shares every month without paying too much attention to what the price is specifically on the day you purchase. In any case, as an investor, you'll simply buy the shares at $30.

As a trader, you're hoping to cash in on the moves of XYZ over the following couple of months. You'll buy an options contract, let's say its premium is $0.90 and the strike price is $35. Your cost for the 100 shares is $90.

Then the stock price shoots up to $45. Since it passed the strike price, you can exercise your option to buy the shares at the strike price. You can buy them at $35 for a total price of $3,500. But remember – you're not an investor in for the long haul. You'll immediately unload the shares. You sell the shares for $4,500 and make a $1,000 profit. After considering your premium, your profit is $910. It will go a little bit lower after considering commissions, but you get the idea. The purpose of buying call options is to make fast profits on stocks you think are going to spike.

It's hard to guess when the best time is to really buy call options. Obviously, you don't want to do it when a major recession hit. The optimal time is during a bull market, or when a specific company is expected to hit on something big, that will suddenly increase its value in the markets. A good time to look is also when a recession hits, but it passes the bottom out period.

5. Option Strategies

A call option is an agreement that gives the financial specialist the privilege to purchase a specific measure of offers (regularly 100 for every agreement) of a specific security or item at a predefined cost over a specific measure of time. For instance, a call option would enable a dealer to purchase a specific measure of portions of either stock, bonds, or even different instruments like ETFs or lists at a later time (by the termination of the agreement).

In case you're purchasing call options, it implies you need the stock (or other security) to go up in cost with the goal that you can make a benefit off of your agreement by practicing your entitlement to purchase those stocks (and frequently, quickly offer them to capitalize on the benefit).

The expense you are paying to purchase the call options is known as the top-notch (it's basically the expense of purchasing the agreement, which will enable you to in the end to purchase the stock or security). In this sense, the premium of the call alternative is similar to an upfront installment like you would put on a house or vehicle. When buying a call, alternatively, you concur with the dealer on a strike cost and are given the options to purchase the security at a foreordained value (which doesn't change until the agreement terminates).

Be that as it may, for what reason would a financial specialist use alternatives? All things considered, purchasing options is fundamentally wagering on stocks to go up, down, or to support an exchanging position in the market.

The cost at which you consent to purchase the fundamental security by means of the alternative is known as the "strike cost," and the expense you pay for purchasing that options agreement is known as the "superior." When deciding the strike value, you are wagering that the advantage (ordinarily a stock) will go up or down in cost. The value you are paying for that wagered is the top-notch, which is a level of the estimation of that benefit.

Why buy Call Options

A call option is an agreement that gives the speculator the privilege to purchase a specific measure of offers (ordinarily 100 for each agreement) of a specific security or product at a predefined cost over a specific measure of time. For instance, a call options would enable a dealer to purchase a specific measure of portions of either stocks, bonds, or even different instruments like ETFs or records at a later time (by the termination of the agreement).

In case you're purchasing a call options, it implies you need the stock (or other security) to go up in cost with the goal that you can make a benefit off of your agreement by practicing your entitlement to purchase those stocks (and for the most part, promptly offer them to capitalize on the benefit).

The expense you are paying to purchase the call alternative is known as the excellent (it's basically the expense of purchasing the agreement which will enable you to in the long run purchase the stock or security). In this sense, the premium of the call alternative is similar to an upfront installment like you would put on a house or vehicle. When buying a call options, you concur with the dealer on a strike cost, and are given the alternative to purchase the security at a foreordained value (which doesn't change until the agreement lapses).

Thus, call alternatives are additionally a lot like protection - you are paying for an agreement that terminates at a set time, yet enables you to buy a security (like a stock) at a foreordained value (which won't go up regardless of whether the cost of the stock available does). In any case, you should reestablish your options (commonly on a week after week, month to month or quarterly premise). Thus, alternatives are continually encountering what's called time rot - which means their worth rots after some time.

For call options, the lower the strike value, the more inherent worth the call alternative has.

Put Options

A put option can be compared to an insurance policy. Say, you just bought a nice car, but you know the risks associated with owning a car. A lot of things can happen to that car. Therefore, you decided to purchase vehicle insurance to protect you against any accidental damage to your home. Either monthly or yearly, you will be required to pay an insurance premium to activate your insurance package. In this case, the insurance has a face value and gives you protection when the car should have an accident.

Consider your stock in ABC Company as the insurance. Instead of securing your vehicle, you're rather securing your stock investment against potential loses. For example, a stock investor may fear that one of his stock portfolios will lose more than 10% of their long position in the market. To hedge against the losses, they buy a put option.

If the stock is selling at 1,500 per share, you can then buy a put option that is going to allow you the to sell a share at $ 1,250 during the specified term of the put contract. Let's say within the six month period, you successfully sold your put option to another options trader at $ 1,250.00 for 100 shares.

Then two months , your stock predictions came through. In this case, you have earned $ 250 for the 100 shares that will be sold. This enables you to make $ 25,000 overall on the entire transaction. If the market value of the share doesn't drop, the only thing you will lose is the initial premium paid for the put option. This example might be overly simple, but you will get the basics of how a put option works.

Typically, the high the strike price of the put option, the greater the intrinsic value of the underlying stock. And an intrinsic value of a share is not dependent on the market value of the share. Intrinsic is usually used by investors using fundamental investing to invest in a stock for a long term to obtain dividends, without worrying too much about the volatility of share value in the market value.

Why to buy Put Options

A put alternative is an agreement that gives the speculator the privilege to sell a specific measure of offers (once more, regularly 100 for each agreement) of a specific security or ware at a predefined cost over a specific measure of time. Much the same as call options, a put options permits the broker the right (however not commitment) to sell a security by the agreement's termination date.

Much the same as call options, the cost at which you consent to sell the stock is known as the strike cost, and the premium is the expense you are paying for the put alternative.

Put options work likewise to calls, with the exception that you need the security to drop in cost in the event that you are purchasing a taken care of alternative to make a benefit (or sell the put options on the off chance that you figure the cost will go up).

On the in spite of call options, with put alternatives, the higher the strike value, the more natural worth the put options has.

6.   More Advanced Strategies

The Call Backspread

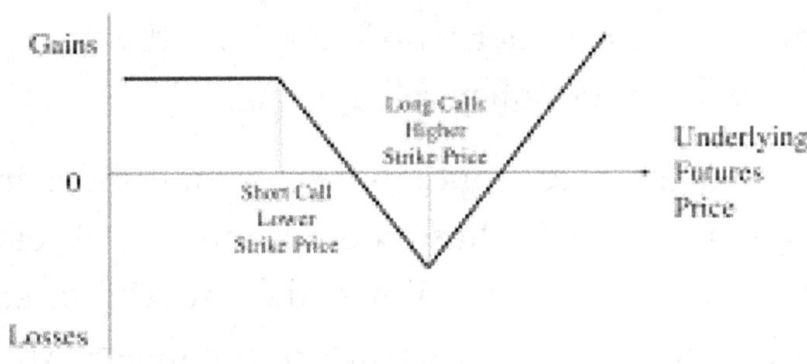

Call Backspread

The backspread is an options strategy that traders take up when they perceive that the market will be very volatile, though not 100% sure on the direction of the price. The stock's significant movement in the preferred direction earns them a big profit, but if it only moves a little, the trader earns a little profit. If the stock fails to move at all, the trader suffers a loss. Backspreads are also called reverse ratio spreads because they are designed to behave in the opposite direction of the ratio spreads.

When you are bullish on a particular stock, the backspread position you take is called the call ratio backspread, or simply, the call backspread. You enter this position when you buy a particular number of out-of-the-money call options (the kind whose strike price is more than stock value), and selling a smaller number of in-the-money call options (current stock price higher than the strike price). You have the liberty to choose the number of call options to sell or buy, but for now, let's only work with the case of a trader who buys 2 on-the-money call options then sells 1 in-the-money call option.

From buying the 2 call options and selling the 1 in-the-money call option, the trader has entered into what is called a credit position. This position allows the trader to earn a premium just by opening a call backspread. It happens when the trader buys the two call options, but since he is not willing to wait for the option to expire, he sells one option. However, even after the sale, the option owner still needs to buy back the option before it expires. These exchanges are what make taking this position quite risky.

If the stock price falls below the call option's strike price sold by the trader, then trader can allow the option to expire because, at this time, both strike prices are now meaningless. When this happens, the profit collected is the initial premium the trader made when he opened the position.

If the price of the stock rises high above the price of the strike price (in-the-money), but it is still below the strike price of the 2 calls, that the trader bought at the on-the-money price, the situation is no longer functional. The 2 calls purchased on-the-money would become worthless, but the call the trader sold at the in-the-money strike price would still be worth something. It will need to be repurchased before the contract expires.

Once the stock price has risen above the in-the-money strike price, the profits you can receive are limitless. The value of the in-the-money call rises, and even then, it must be repurchased. The cost of purchasing the option, however, will be negated by the trader's possession of the 2 calls he bought at the in-the-money strike price. What's more, the two calls' value will be rising quickly, and the trader can sell them at a profit.

As a put, the backspread functions the same way, only in the opposite direction, in a bearish position.

Kindly remember that when it comes to the backspread position, you cannot allow your contracts to expire because the options you will have sold will need to be repurchased to keep them from being exercised. As such, before you settle for the backspread, ensure that you have enough money to buy back the options in the event, the stock price fails to move.

The Synthetic Short Stock

The synthetic short stock is an options trading strategy that takes the form of buying or selling a stock, but with call or put options.

In a typical situation where a trader only buys the primary put option, no profits would be realized until the stock price begins to fall under the strike price a bit. On the other hand, if the investor decides to invest in put options, he would have to pay the full premium, with the maximum possible loss being that premium.

In the case of the synthetic short stock, however, a trader can begin to enjoy some profits, once the stock price falls under the strike price, and the amount made after selling the corresponding call option makes up for the premium the trader spends buying the put option.

The advantages of the synthetic short stock strategy come with a big pay-off, unfortunately. The trader is now exposed to unlimited losses. For example, the more and more the value of the stock increases, the more the money the investor needs to buy back his call option before it expires. This makes taking this position very expensive, especially if the trader had made a faulty prediction concerning the likely direction of the stock.

The opposite of the synthetic short stock is the synthetic long stock. It behaves in a directly opposite behavior and is used by traders who feel bullish about their position to a stock.

That said, the synthetic stock strategies are thought to be excellent low-cost ways of dealing with basic options because their premiums are often offset once the trader sells the option under the opposite contract. However, this setup is seen to be almost similar to futures trading, and the thing with futures is that a wrong prediction could end up being too costly, just as we see with the synthetics.

The Long Butterfly Spread

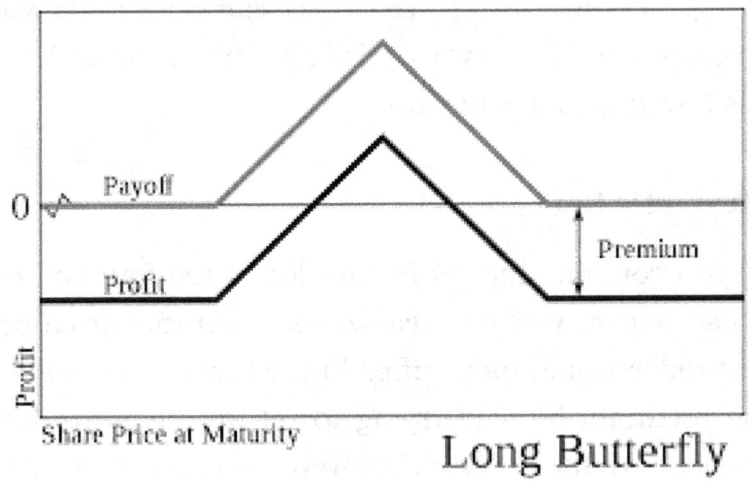

The Butterfly spread strategy is composed of 2 vertical spreads with an everyday strike price. The two spreads are the initial position where options are bought or sold, at 3 individual strike prices. These calls can be either calls or puts. The arrangement of the options makes the Butterfly spread a strategy that limits both profits and losses.

There is no difference between a Long Butterfly spread created with either calls or puts because, due to put-call parity, a Long Butterfly spread created out of put options behaves precisely like one created out of call options. Therefore, whichever you use, calls, or puts, you can create a Long Butterfly.

Take the example of a trader who purchases 1 in-the-money call option but sells 2 at-the-money call options, before purchasing another out-of-the-money call option. As you see, this strategy combines two opposing vertical spread options, which is how it got its name, the

Butterfly Spread

If you combine the profit profiles of the four call options mentioned above, you will realize that was the strike price to fall, the trader would only suffer limited losses. He would only lose the premium he paid trying to set up the entire butterfly arrangement. If the stock price were to climb very high, the losses would be limited too. However, if the stock price remained around the at-the-money strike price, the trader would receive some profit, but it too would be limited.

The Long Butterfly is thus a comfortably neutral strategy for when the market is experiencing low volatility because the trader will be making a correct bet, saying that the stock price would not be making much movement. Then he would receive the maximum profits, the limited ones we mentioned above.

Another advantage of the Butterfly strategy is that it is a low-risk approach. In case the stock climbs unexpectedly or crashes, the losses suffered will be limited.

The Short Butterfly strategy is just like the Long Butterfly strategy, but the roles are reversed. Its spreads are reversed, and it is taken up when the market is experiencing volatile shocks.

One keynote you ought to make regarding the Butterfly positions is that they involve three different strike prices, whether buying or selling options. To take it up, most brokers will ask you to pay 3 commissions to open the position, and you must pay 3 more commissions as you exit. Therefore, keep these commissions in mind when weighing the possibility of taking the Butterfly. See whether it will be a profitable strategy, given your circumstances.

7. The Long Iron Condor

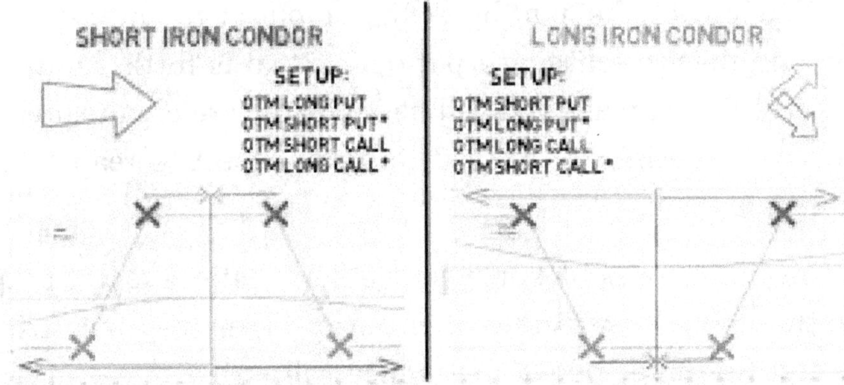

The Iron Condor strategies are an advanced strategy that, just like the Butterfly, uses two vertical spreads. The trader opens a call spread at a strike price higher than the current stock value of the underlying asset and opens a put spread too, at a strike price that is lower than the current stock value.

Of the Iron Condor strategies, the Long Iron Condor is the most popular, and it is also one of the most preferred advanced options buying strategies. Options trading instructors highly recommend it.

Using the Long Iron Condor strategy is similar to making a 'sure bet' although it leaves room for some modest profit and a few errors. The strategy is designed to be used on stocks that are not volatile, and those that maintain a neutral trading range. In addition, in case the stock price moves too much and the option reaches its expiration date, the losses resulting from this are very high, although limited.

You create the put by selling 1 out-of-the-money put option and then purchasing 1 put option that is further out-of-the-money. The spreads you will have created are credit spread, and once the position is opened, you can expect to reap some income from them.

Having this unique spreads together creates a target price range that falls between the inner out-of-the-money put strike price and the inner out-of-the-money call strike price. In the event the underlying stock price stays around this range by the time the expiry date comes, all four options will become worthless, and you get to keep the credit income you had at the start. If, however, the performance of the underlying stock becomes more volatile than you hoped and even gets out of the price range, you must close your in-the-money positions immediately. Unfortunately, doing this will reduce your profits and in the end, bring you a net loss.

In comparison to other neutral trading strategies, the Long Iron Condor stands out. If you compared it to similar strategies that deal with non-volatile stocks like the Strong Strangle and the Long Butterfly, you would note the differences. For example, if the price changes drastically, a trader using the Strong Strangle will suffer unlimited loss while a trader using the Long Iron Condor will only experience some limited maximum losses.

If the stock price remains at the same position without any movement, under the Long Butterfly, the trader will enjoy a maximum profit. However, the Long Iron Condor makes more room, with its more extensive price range, within which the trader can enjoy the maximum profit. This price range can be controlled too. If you make it narrower, you make room to receive more initial credit income, but this exposes you to the risk of having the stock price landing out of this range.

One significant disadvantage of the Long Iron Condor strategy is that it is made up of four individual options, and this could translate to higher commission costs, depending on the policies of your broker, in comparison to other strategies. What's more, the maximum loss potential that a trader stands to incur is often more than the initial credit income the trader placed when opening this position. These two factors are substantial, and they make the Long Iron Condor appear less profitable than people presume it to be. Therefore, before you take it up, it would serve you well to sit down and analyze all factors involved, weigh out the situation effectively, and see whether the strategy is appropriate for your trading goals. Do not forget to include the commission costs in your analysis.

The Short Iron Condor works in the opposite direction, and it is best suited for volatile stocks.

The Long Strangle

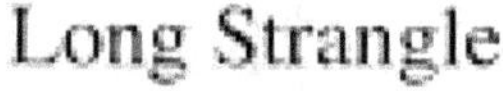

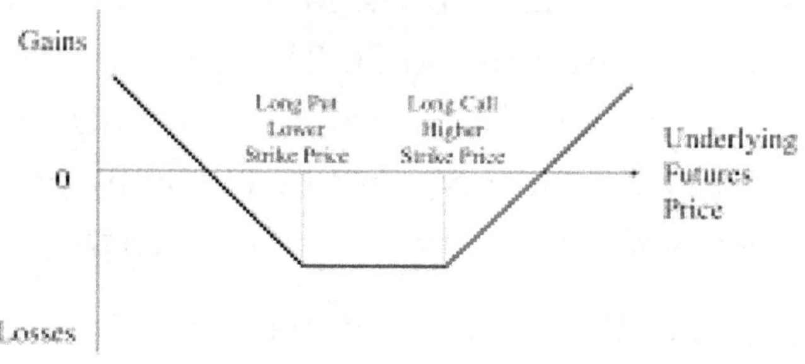

Strangle strategy options are strategies that thrive enable the trader's investments to thrive when the stock is volatile. The long strangle, for example, is the position a trader takes when anticipating high volatility in the underlying stock. The trader creates the Long Strangle position by purchasing 1 out-of-the-money call option, and 1 out-of-the-money put option. These options must share an expiration date.

Although the call option's stock price will be below the strike price, the call will not be worth anything, but once that stock price goes beyond the strike price, the call option will produce some profit. In the same way, the put option will be worthless so long as the stock price is above the option's strike price. However, once the strike price is higher than the stock price, the put option will begin to give some value.

When a trader brings together the two different profiles of the call and puts options, the result is the Long Strangle position. This strategy gives the trader the potential to make unlimited profits as the stock price climbs higher or falls lower. However, if the stock value stays within the confines of the two strike prices, both options will be rendered worthless, bringing a loss to the investment portfolio.

You ought to close your Long Strangle position before the expiry date of the options comes. You can do this by selling the option leg that has value and let the other option leg expire (expiry saves you some commission or fees charged when you transact). Therefore, if you realize that the stock has climbed, sell that call option and allow the put option to expire. If the stock price has fallen, expect the opposite. If the stock price remained stationary, you have to allow both options to expire, or if they have any time value left, you could sell them.

As we have mentioned, the Long Strangle is suitable for volatile stocks, those that you are sure will have dramatic climbs or falls in the future. This is a suitable strategy for when you are waiting for some big financial statement to be made, such as when a company is about to report on the performance of its stocks. If the performance has been excellent, the stock price will skyrocket, but if the performance were terrible, the price would plummet. Other pieces of news that could cause volatility include the resolution of a lawsuit, the release of some research results, and a change of monetary or fiscal policy.

When it comes to strategy and execution, the Short Strangle is the Long Strangle is the exact opposite. The Short Strangle is best suited for stocks whose prices remain still and do not fluctuate. This makes it one of the neutral strategies that traders take up to reap profits out of very little if any, market activity.

8.　Broker and Commission

Once you decide to invest in option trading and you get the necessary in formation, the following step will involve choosing a suitable broker. Perhaps you do not know what a broker is. Well, a broker acts as an intermediary while carrying out a trade. We have brokers that deal with clients directly and some that that act as a link between the more prominent broker and the client. All are essential while carrying out a trade. While selecting a suitable broker, here are some factors that you can consider

The cost

The topic on cost happens to be quite controversial. There are some who will advise you to get a cheap broker and some will advise you to get a broker that charges more. At the same time, you will have some telling you to work with your budget. When it comes to determining the cost of services, there are a number of factors that can be considered. Some who have had a more significant exposure and years of experience in a certain field can regard themselves as experts and they have the right to do so. You will find that most of them will charge high fees for the services that they offer since they believe that they can give you value for your money.

The good thing is; there are some who are able to do this.

On the other hand, you will come across some who are new in the industry. They may have all the necessary information but they happen to lack the necessary years of experience. Their rates may be low, but that does not mean that they cannot help in your investments. Personally, I would advise you to work within your budget as you decide on the best broker.

Trading platform

While trading options, most of the activities will be carried out in the brokers trading platform. The trading platforms are at times referred to as brokerage accounts. You need to properly evaluate the brokerage accounts of the various brokers before engaging them. As the option trading industry expands, it has sparked a lot of interest among individuals. We have had more brokers getting in the market and more trading platforms being established daily. Some of these trading platforms are a true definition of a pure scam. They happen to have unfavorable terms that cannot benefit the trader in any way. Most have been established by greedy people who are just after earning an extra coin and have little or no consideration for other people. The trading platform will tell you more about the kind of broker that you are dealing with.

It you notice anything alarming, that should send you a message to make you avoid that particular broker.

Remember that this is an investment that you will be making. Anywhere you decide to put your finances, you have to ensure that they are safe and secure so that you do not end up making a loss. While checking the brokers trading platform, be careful to look at what other people have to say regarding that platform. The internet came to make life easier for us. With the help of a single click you can learn a lot about something or someone. Get to see the ratings and checks of that particular trading platform. When the checks are positive, you can be confident that you are investing your finances in the right broker. On the other hand, when the checks are negative, it should act as a warning to avoid the broker.

Investment style

Are you a buy and hold investor or a trader?

Your response towards this question can tell a lot about the kind of broker that you should be looking for. Different investment styles require different brokers. The broker that may work for a particular investment may fail terribly in another investment. Traders are mainly short term investors. They rely on earning profits within a short duration of time. Based on the trade markets, the investment can take a short or long time before it brings capital gain. However, the duration is not the same as it would take a buy and hold investor.

Since trade is a short time investment, there are many risks that a trader is likely to encounter while carrying out the trade. He or she requires a good broker so as to avoid the losses that may be incurred from making wrong and uninformed trade decisions. To avoid the possibility of incurring negative returns, one has to invest in a good broker. The buy and hold investor makes a long term investment. It involves holding goods until the period they can earn maximum profits. In both cases, a good broker is required.

Do some research

Before engaging any broker, it is advisable that you do some background check. There are a lot of findings that you can come across while doing your research. The discoveries will tell you a lot regarding the type of broker that you are dealing with. It is a good thing that the resources we need are easily accessible. The internet is one good place to confirm if your doubts are true. Utilize it well to find out as many things as you can. While doing so, do not ignore any information that you come across. Everything that you learn is important and essential while selecting the right broker. Some people say that it is important to look at the experience of the broker.

I wouldn't disagree with that fact is experience is very important. A broker who has worked for ten years in that field is better placed than one who has worked for a year or to. Chances are; they have picked up a lot of information and tactics along the way. However, human ability is not limited by time. A broker may be green in the field, but work their way up in being the best broker around. It all depends on the commitment one has towards making their business a success.

Factors to Consider When Selecting A Brokerage Account

Commission and rates

Different brokerage accounts charge different rates and commissions depending on the broker. When it comes to the commissions charged, try to avoid those with high commissions. When conducting a trade, there is a certain profit or loss that you can incur. When you make a profit, the brokerage account can take up some commission. If it takes up high commission, it limits the amount of money that you earn from a particular trade. It is better if you select a brokerage account that charges low commission. Asides from the commission, there are other rates that may be involved in a brokerage account. Before getting the account, carry out a proper search on those rates. Learn how they can influence your earning. This can be in a positive or a negative way. If you want to generate an income form trading option, then you will look for accounts with favorable rates. While looking at the rates, also consider the trading costs of that particular account. This information will help you in making the right decision.

Market access

The choice on market access is determined by the type of trader that you are. If you would like to be a small scale trader, you can focus on the local markets. On the same note, if you would like to be a large scale trader, you can focus on the international market. Different brokerage accounts have different market access. There are some that focus on the local market. Such accounts tend to be limiting in terms of the income one is likely to earn. For anyone aspiring to earn a fortune from the option trading market, this is not a suitable account for them. Such an account can be a good start for beginners who are fresh in the trading industry. It can act as a good start up point as they learn how to make it in the industry. For the heavy investors, the best platform would be one that offers access to the international market.

There are plenty of opportunities that the investor can decide to indulge in. The available options are many, and the investor can choose the option that best suits them. Be keen while selecting the best brokerage account based on market access.

Investment insight

Some brokerage accounts offer tips to the account owners, on how they can trade to get successful outcomes. All this tips are essential in the success of a trader. This shows that the service provider cares about the development of the investor and as a result, they keep educating them to allow them to become better at what they do. While selecting a brokerage account, it is important to get an account that cares for the needs of the investors. Look at an account that can enhance your growth. There are some brokerage accounts that offer extra services by providing the graphs and charts that enable you to analyze the market movement.

This information helps you know when to trade and when to avoid trading. Most of the trading mistakes most people make result from lack of knowledge. You find that a trader has no clue on how the trade market is moving yet, they are engaging in the trade.

Avoid finding yourself in such situations by making the informed decision while selecting your brokerage account. Be keen to select the accounts that provide extra services that facilitate your growth in option trading.

Ensure that your data is secure

Data security is one thing that you need to consider while selecting a brokerage account. There is a lot of personal information that you get to fill in while opening a brokerage account. You have to ensure that is information is protected and that it is not used anywhere against your will.

We have had cases of companies misusing personal data for selfish gains. As a result, they endanger people by exposing their personal data. As a wise investor this is a serious factor to put into consideration. While checking the background of various brokerage accounts, ensure that the one you select has the best policies. Some companies offer guarantee that they will protect your investment and ensure that your information is well guarded. You can know if a company stays true to their word by looking at their checks. In case you come across some complains that they misuse the clients' data, then that should act as a warning sign to avoid such companies. If at all you do not come across such checks, then you can be confident that the company is a safe place to trade.

The customer service provided

You require a brokerage account that provides the best customer service. The type of service provided by a company, can tell you a lot about that particular company. If you notice some challenges in their mode of communicating with their clients, that should act as a red flag in avoiding to invest in that particular brokerage account. You can know the type of services rendered by the brokerage account by evaluating the checks provided by the users. This is one of the best ways to find out more about the company and how it treats its clients. Negative checks should make you avoid engaging in that brokerage account. On the other hand, positive checks should encourage you to engage in a particular brokerage accounts. It is sad that some companies provide fabricated checks that may be misguiding the public. While selecting the best brokerage account, consider getting referrals from people that you know. It is better than getting the advice online, since you have proof that what is being said is right. While trading, there are some questions that may arise and you would like to seek answers to the questions. You need a brokerage account that offers a support system to answer such questions.

9.   Get Started

Day Trade Rules

Day trading involves making quick decisions. This explains why you must always have your emotions under control. If you fail to control them, you may lose any profits and capital accumulated over time in a single trade gone wrong.

When most traders lose part of their capital to some trades, they tend to get frustrated and fearful. This causes them to over-leverage the little money remaining. As a result, they end up blowing their account in one or a few risky trades. Day trading is not like other long-term trading strategies where you can quickly determine the direction of market prices. That is why you need to stick to your initial plan and strategy.

One of the attributes that make day traders remain in business is discipline. The strategy demands a lot of concentration and focus. You must, therefore, seek to understand how best to control your emotions when trading. Let us look at some of the things you need to do to avoid emotional trading:

- **Avoid less volatile trading seasons**. Most day traders prefer trading during sessions of high volatility. This sometimes leads to congestion in the marketplace, and if you do not have the right skills and strategies, you may end up frustrated. If the market gets flooded and the prices seem stagnant, avoid entering any positions as this can result in tremendous losses.

- **Exit the market after a few wins.** Once you make three or more consecutive wins, stop trading until another time. This also applies to losing. When you win consecutively, you may start feeling that you are a super trader. In such excitement, you can end up entering the wrong trades, thus losing all your profits. Most people revenge trade as a way of recovering what they have already lost. This results in more losses. Therefore, you should exit the market for a few minutes or hours when you consistently win or lose.

- **Take a break between trades.** Given the rapid changes in market prices when day trading, it is easy for you to get drowned into the trade and forget about your emotions. You must take a break from the trading platform after each trade. This will give you time to reflect on the following move you need to make and give you better control of your emotions.

- **Don't focus on the outcome.** To keep your emotions in check, avoid checking your losses and profits when trading. If you do this, you will definitely experience a surge of emotions that may be difficult to control. Always stick to the rules of trade as you hope to gain some profit at the end of the day.

As you do the above, you must bear in mind that controlling your emotions needs a lot of patience and perseverance. You must keep improving on your emotional stability for the long-term success of your business. With time, you will realize that you do not need to concentrate on managing any emotions. You would have rained your brain to respond to the various emotional triggers.

10. Swing Trade Rules

Swing Trading is a momentary stock trading style. You take little benefits, and cut misfortunes snappier. To make it work, your principles for trading should be specific to the shorter period. In spite of the fact that the additions may be littler, the shorter holding time frame implies you can intensify your increases into huge benefits after some time. Here are the essentials of executing a swing trading system.

- Always align your **trade** with the overall direction of the market. ...

- Go long strength. ...

- Never **trade** only on the short-term chart of the **swing-trading** time frame. ...

- Try to enter the **trade** near the beginning of the trend, not near the end.

Selling Call Options

You might ask why someone would sell a call option in the first place since they can end up having to sell shares of stock. The reason is that selling options is a way to generate monthly income. As we will see , if you already own shares of stock, you can sell options contracts against them and earn money from the sale. Owners of shares of stock that do this are making a bet that they can sell the options contract and earn money without having to sell their shares, but if you decide to sell options contracts be aware that in some cases the right to buy the shares will be exercised. So while you will profit from the premium you earned from the sale of the options contract, you may be forced to sell your shares of stock.

Advanced options traders can sell options contracts without having actually to own the shares of stock. The danger is that the owner of the option (the buyer) will exercise it.

In that case, the seller of the naked call will lose money, because they would have to buy the shares of stock at the market price, and then sell them to the owner of the options contract at the lower strike price. So they would lose the difference: (market price – strike price + premium paid per share) x 100 shares.

If the party who writes the options contract owns the share of stock, it's best to enter into this type of arrangement when you can set a high strike price. In other words, choose a price that is higher than the price you originally paid to obtain the shares. That way even though you might be forced to sell the shares, at least you will make a profit on the deal. However, you won't make as much profit as you could have had you sold the shares on the open market. We say that you missed out on the upside.

In the end, selling options contracts is a bet against the stock, in the sense that you don't think the share price is going to go as high as the buyer believes it will go. If it fails to do so, the option will reach the expiration date, and it will "expire worthless" because nobody would buy shares that were more expensive than the going rate.

Call options have this name because the originator of the options contract might have to sell the shares of stock that they own; in other words, the shares will be "called away."

Covered Call

If you have 100 or more shares of a particular stock, you can sell covered calls against your shares. This is a common strategy used by people to earn money off their shares, but you always face the risk that your shares will be called away if the option is exercised. One strategy that can be used is to sell out of the money calls when you don't expect the share price to rise to the strike price of the call option over the lifetime of the contract.

For example, Facebook is trading at $190.25 a share. You can sell a $210 call for $0.64, so for all 100 shares, one option contract would net you $64. This is for an expiration date in 30 days. Or you could take a higher level of risk and sell a $195 call for $4.05, which would give you a premium of $405 per option contract. If you had 500 shares, then you'd receive $2,025 in premiums. Not a bad passive income and all you have to do is hope that the share price stays below the strike price.

If the share price closes in on the strike price, then you will be faced with a dilemma – risk having the option exercised if the share price rises above the strike price or you can buy back the option and cut into your profits. With a few days left to expiration, the option you sold may be worth $2.05, so you could buy back the five options you sold, and you'd reduce your net profit to $1,000.

You could go further out, even selling LEAPS. In that case, the premium paid is much larger. A Facebook LEAP with a $195 call that expires in 18 months has a premium of $30.58, so selling five contracts for your 500 shares could bring in an income of $15,290. Of course, there is a higher risk that the share price will rise above the strike price over an 18 month period than there is over the short term.

The one principle to keep in mind selling covered calls is that you could lose your shares if the option is exercised. With that in mind, you should only select a strike price that is of higher amount than what you had paid for the shares. That way if you are forced to sell the shares, then you are not taking a loss doing so. That can make losing the shares easier to deal with. So if we had purchased our shares at $200 a share, we would not select a $195 strike price because that represents a potential loss, which would be given by the price we paid for the shares minus the strike price and then less the premium aid, in this case $200 - $195 - $4.05 so we'd end up losing $0.95 on the trade. If you had purchased the shares at a lower price, say $190 a share, then the $195 strike would make sense since if the stock price rose and the shares were called away, we'd still profit by selling the shares.

Protected puts are the put version of a covered call. The risk with a protected put is that the shares will be "put to you" and you will have to buy the shares, so you will be required to have enough capital in your account in order to cover the purchase.

Of course, the trick to selling options is to pick a strike price where you think the option will expire worthlessly. There is always the risk that you are wrong, but if you think the share price is going to rise for Facebook, to use an example, you could sell a protected $190 put for $4.95, earning $495 per contract. If the share price rises, the options would expire worthlessly, and you would keep the premium and profit from the deal.

11. Debit Spread

A debit spread is a method that is similar to buying a call or a put but in exchange for limiting the potential gains you can get from a trade, the probability of earning a profit is higher. The first debit spread that we are going to consider is called a call debit spread. The motivation for using a call debit spread is similar to buying a call option by itself. This is done in the belief that the share price of the stock is going to rise before the options expire.

With a called debit spread you buy and sell to call options at the same time. Depending on your broker you may have to be a level III options trader in order to execute this strategy. The reason is it involves selling an option. Second of all even though the option is being sold as part of a larger strategy, it's not going to be backed with anything and so could possibly cause some trouble which we will discuss .

For call debit spread you have to call options and they will both have the same expiration date. However, they're going to have different strike prices. This mitigates your risk a little bit because by selling a call option you are going to receive a payment. A call debit spread is a debit, because you are going to purchase a more expensive call option with a lower strike price, and you're going to sell a lower-priced call option with a higher strike price. So the call option that you sell is going to partially offset the cost of the more expensive call option that you purchase.

The first thing to pay attention to what the debit spread is the break even price. For call debit spread, the break even price is the lower strike price plus the debit that was required to enter the position. So if you buy a call option with a $100 strike price that costs three dollars, and you sell a call option was $110 strike price for one dollar, first you calculate the difference between the premiums paid. So you've subtracted the premium for the higher strike price which is one dollar, from the premium you paid for the lower strike price which is $3. So that's $3-$1=$2. Then you add this to the lower strike price to get the break even. In this case that would be $100 +$2 =$102. That means the share price has to rise to $102 before you have a chance of seeing a profit on the deal. You will make money as long as the stock is in the range of the break even price up to the offer strike price. So in our example, as long as the share price ends up between $102 and $110, we can make a profit. If the price rises above $110, the gain is fixed but no longer increases. For a call debit spread, the possible profit is the difference in the strike prices minus the price paid to enter the position. In this example, the difference in the strike prices is $10, and the debit is $2, so the maximum profit is $8. That is on a per-share basis, so with 100 shares, it's $800.

To see the benefits of what the structure of the call debit spread can do here is an actual example of a Netflix debit spread. The lower strike price is $402.50. The cost to enter the position is $2.37. So the break even point is $404.87. Slightly above the break-even price, it would make a profit of a couple of hundred dollars. But the higher above the break even price, the higher the gain to a point. This one hits a gain of $2013 when it reaches the higher strike price of $425. If the price goes anything above that even $500 we won't see any more profits from the position.

Credit Spread

A Credit Spread is a short spread strategy in which you get the premium of the option you sold as credit in your account. You can create a Credit Spread position by selling an option contract of a strike price that is closer to the underlying price and by buying an option contract of a strike price which is further away from the underlying price. Because the nearer strike price has more premium than the farther strike price, the position will create a net credit in your account. Both options of the position should be of the same type (either a Call or Put) and also of same maturity. And, in a regular Credit Spread, quantities of both options should be same.

Selling naked Put Options

Selling naked puts is a popular strategy for traders that are given level 4 status. If you can get this level from your broker, you can consider this possibly profitable strategy. Of course, the key is choosing the right strike price.

When a put is "naked," that means it isn't backed by anything. However, you are still required by law to fulfill your obligations should the option be exercised, but one way that traders avoid this problem is by buying the options back if there is a chance they would be exercised. Time value may work in your favor, which will make the options cheaper and so you can buy them back and still profit.

Another consideration is to choose a relatively low implied volatility, which reduces the chances that the stock will move much over the lifetime of the option. But that is a trade-off as well, as implied volatility that is a few points higher can result in a large increase in the premium received for selling the option.

Consider IBM. The stock price is at $139.20, but you could sell a 30 day $135 put for $2.44, or $244. You could even sell in the money puts. A $145 put would sell for $748 if you sold five contracts that would be a 30-day income of $3,640.

Selling in the money puts could be risky, but beneficial if it was believed that IBM shares were set to rise in price. If the price rises above the strike price, then the options will expire worthlessly.

Selling LEAPS, while it carries higher risk since a long time to expiration gives a higher probability that the option will move in the amount, also allow you to sell at high premiums. A $130 put for IBM expiring in 18 months would sell for $13.20, so selling five contracts would give you a premium of $6,600. Bid-Ask spreads can be large for LEAPS, and the volume is probably small. For this particular option, we find that the bid-ask spread is about 80 cents, which isn't too bad meaning selling it might not be that difficult. Daily volume is small at 10, but the open interest is 1,282. Experienced traders often recommend an open interest of 500 or higher since that indicates there are enough people buying the contracts.

The risk with naked puts is that you will be forced to buy the shares. Again, if it looks like that might turn out to be the case, you can buy the contracts back. Selling out of the money options that expire in the near term can leave you in a better position since the options will probably expire worthlessly, and you will be able to keep the premium without having to buy back the options. If you have to buy the shares, the loss would be the share price minus the market price. But of course, you'd have to get the capital to buy the shares as well.

So if you sold a put option on IBM with a strike price of $138 expiring in 6 weeks, it would sell for $3.70. If the share price dropped to $136, you'd have to use cash to buy the shares at $138, and possibly lose $2 a share by selling them – or you could simply keep them and wait for the price to go back up. Plus your loss would be offset by the premium, so your break-even point is the amount of the strike price minus the premium paid.

12. Trading Psychology

We associate trading psychology to some behaviors and emotions that are often the triggers for catalysts for decisions. The most common emotions that every trader will come across is fear and greed.

Fear

At any given time, fear represents one of the worst kinds of emotions that you can have. Check in your newspaper one day, and you read about a steep selloff, and the following thing is trying to rack your brain about what to do following even if it isn't the right action at that time.

Many investors think that they know what will happen in the following few days, which makes them have a lot of confidence in the outcome of the trade. This leads to investors getting into the trade at a level that is too high or too low, which in turn makes them react emotionally.

As the trader puts a lot of hope on the single trade, the level of fear tends to increase, and hesitation and caution kick in.

Fear is part of every trader, but skilled traders have the capacity to manage the fear. There are various types of fears that you will experience, let us look at a few of them:

The Fear to Lose

Have you ever entered a trade and all you could think about is losing? The fear of losing makes it hard for you to execute the perfect strategy or enter or exit a strategy at the right time.

As a trader, you know that you need to make timely decisions when the strategy signals you to take one. When you have fear guiding you, the level of confidence drops, and you don't have the ability to execute the strategy the right way, at the right time. When a strategy fails, you lose trust in your abilities as well as strategy.

When you lose trust in many of the strategies, you end up with analysis paralysis, whereby you don't have the capacity to pull the trigger on any decision that you make. Making a move becomes a huge challenge.

When you cannot pull the trigger, all you can think about is staying away from the pain of losing, while you need to move towards gains.

No trader likes to lose, but it is a fact that even the best traders will make losses once in a while. The key is for them to make more profitable trades that allow them to stay in the game.

When you worry too much, you end up being distracted from your execution process, and instead, you focus on the results.

To reduce the fear in trading, you need to accept losses. The probability of losing or making a profit is 50/50, and you need to accept this fact and accept a trade, whether it is a sell or a buy signal.

The Fear of a Positive Trend Going Negative (and Vice Versa)

Many traders choose to go for quick profits and then leave the losses to run down. Many traders want to convince themselves that they have made some money for the day, so they tend to go for a quick profit so that they have the winning feeling.

So, what should you do instead? You need to stick with the trend. When you notice a trend is starting, it is good to stay with the trend until you have a signal that the trend is about to reverse. It is only then that you exit this position.

To understand this concept, you need to consider the history of the market. History is good at pointing out that times change, and trends can go either way. Remember that no one knows the exact time the trend will start or end; all you need to do is wait upon the signal.

The Fear of Missing Out

For every trade, you have people that doubt the capacity of the trade to go through. After you place the trade, you will be faced with many skeptics that will doubt the whole procedure and leave you wondering whether to exit the strategy or not.

This fear is also characterized by greed – because you aren't working on the premise of making a successful trade rather the fact that the security is rising without you having a piece of the pie.

This fear is usually based on information that there is a trend which you missed that you would have capitalized on.

This fear has a downside – you will forget about any potential risk associated with the trade and instead think that you have the capacity to make a profit because other people benefited from the action.

Fear of Being Wrong

Many traders put too much emphasis on being right that they forget that this is a business they should run the right way. They also forget that being successful is all about knowing the trend and how it affects their engagement.

When you follow the best timing strategy, you create many positive results over a certain time.

The uncanny desire to focus on always being right instead of focusing on making money is a great part of your ego, and to stay on the right path; you need to trade without your ego for once.

If you accommodate a perfectionist mentality when you get into trades, you will be after failure because you will experience a lot of losses as well. Perfectionists don't take losses the right way, and this translates into fear.

Ways to Overcome Fear in Trading

As you can see, it is obvious that fear can lead to losses. So, how can you avoid this fear and become successful?

Learn

You need to find a way to get knowledge so that you have the basis for making decisions. When you know all there is to know about options, you know what to buy and when to sell, and learn which ones to watch. You are then more comfortable making the right decisions.

Have Goals

What are your short term and long-term goals? Setting the right goals helps you to overcome fear. When you have goals, you have rules that dictate how you behave, even in times of fear. You also have a timeline for your journey.

Envision the Bigger Picture

You always need to evaluate your choices at all times and see what you have gained or lost so far for taking some steps. Understanding the mistakes, you made gives you guidance to make better decisions in the future.

Start Small

Many traders that subscribe to fear have lost a lot before. They put a lot of funds on the line and ended up losing, which in turn made them fear to place other trades. Begin with small sums so that you don't risk too much to put fear in you. Once you get more confident, you can invest larger sums so that you enjoy more profit.

Use the Right Strategy

Having the right trading strategy makes it easy to execute your trades successfully. Make sure you look at various options trading strategies so that you know which one is ideal for your situation and skills.

Many strategies can help you succeed, but others might leave you confused. If you have a strategy that doesn't give you the returns you desire, then adjust it to suit your needs over time. Refine it till you are comfortable with its performance.

Go Simple

When you have a strategy that is simple and straightforward, you will be less likely to lose confidence along the way because you know what to expect.

Additionally, the easier the strategy, the faster it will be to spot any issues.

Don't Hesitate

At times you have to jump into the fray even if you aren't so comfortable with the way it works. Once you begin taking steps, you will learn more about the trade.

However, you need always to be prepared when taking any trade. The more prepared you are, the easier it will be for you to run successful trades.

Don't Give Up

Things might not always go as you expect them to do. Remember that mistakes are there to give you lessons that will make you a better trader. When you lose, take time to identify the mistake you made and then correct it, then try again.

Greed

This refers to a selfish desire to get more money than you need from a trade. When the desire to get more than you can usually make takes over your decision-making process, you are looking at failure.

Greed is seen to be more detrimental than fear. Yes, fear can make you lose trades, but the good thing is that you get to preserve your capital. On the other hand, greed places you in a situation where you spend your capital faster than you return it. It pushes you to act when you shouldn't be acting at all.

The Danger of Being Greedy

When you are greedy, you end up acting irrationally. Irrational trading behavior can be over-trading, over-leveraging, holding onto trades for too long, or chasing different markets.

The more greed you have, the more foolish you act. If you reach a point at which greed takes over from common sense, then you are overdoing it.

When you are greedy, you also end up risking way much more than you can handle and you end up with a loss. You also have unrealistic expectations from the market, which makes it seem as if you are after just money and nothing else.

When you are greedy, you also start trading prematurely without any knowledge of the options trading market.

When you are too greedy, your judgment is clouded, and you won't think about any negative consequences that might result when you make certain decisions.

Many traders that were too greedy ended up giving up after making this mistake in the initial trading phase.

How to Overcome Greed

Like any other endeavors in trading, you need a lot of efforts to overcome greed. It might not be easy because we are talking about human emotions here, but it is possible.

First, you have to know that every call you make won't be the right one at all times. There are times when you won't make the right move, and you will end up losing money. At times you will miss the perfect strategy altogether, and you won't move a step ahead.

Secondly, you have to agree that the market is way bigger than you. When you do this, you will accept and make mistakes in the process.

Hope

Hope is what keeps a trading expectation alive when it has reached reversal. Hope is usually factored in the mind of a trader that has placed a huge amount on a trade. Many traders also go for hope when they wish to recoup past losses. These traders are always hopeful that the following trade will be the best, and they end up placing more than they should on the trade.

This type of emotion is dangerous because the market doesn't care at all about your hopes and will take your money.

Regret

This is the feeling of disappointment or sadness over a trade that has been done, especially when it has resulted in a loss.

Focusing too much on missing on trade makes the trader not to move forward. After you learn the lessons after such a loss, you need to understand the mistakes you made then move ahead.

When you decide to let regret to rule your thinking, you start chasing markets with the hopes that you will end up making money on a position by doubling the entrance price.

13. Risk Management

Risks are part of stock investing or any investment. You cannot avoid these risks, no matter how knowledgeable you are. The only way to deal with these risks is by minimizing your exposure to them. Before you can develop strategies for minimizing your risks, understand them first. You need to know the different types of risks and what factors affect a risk to become a threat to your chances of earning gain.

The Different Kinds of Risks

Risk is losing part or all of the value of the investment. Some risks are directly related while other risks indirectly affect stocks investment and your purchasing power. Risks are inherent to any investment so do not let these risks hinder you from investing your money on stocks.

Financial Risk

Financial risk is a concern even for established companies. This risk refers to the inability of a company to pay its investors. Remember, a company that declares insolvency pays first the creditors before paying shareholders and investors when the company is in the process of liquidation. More often, shareholders might not recover their investment value when the company declares bankruptcy.

Risk related to Interest rate

It is used to show the effect of a hike in interest rate after buying an investment. Oftentimes, this type of risk is directly related to investments that generate liability or investments that require payment of interest payout to investors. An example of liability-generating investment is bonds. Interest rate risk affects the financial condition of a company, especially for companies that rely on debts instruments to raise capitalization.

This risk affects stock investment. When a company issues bonds and other debts instruments and suffers from sudden increased of interest rates, chances are their capacity to pay might be affected. Higher rates mean higher payment of interest. This means the company pays first the creditors before they could pay their investors. As a result, the value of stocks may decrease or dividend payout may be postponed.

With a higher interest rate, stock investors tend to sell their shares, especially in the electric and financial industries. These investors may decide to invest in debt instruments instead of stock investment. To minimize interest risks, expert investors diversify their portfolio by investing in money market instruments that perform and still earn even during high-interest rates.

Market Risk

Market risk refers to the demand and supply movement in the market. When a type of share becomes in demand and its supply becomes limited, its price increases. Conversely, when no investor wants a particular stock, its price decreases. Price and value of stocks increase or decrease depending on market demand. This is the reason stock is a risky investment in a short-term period. The stock market is unpredictable because of the millions of investors buying and selling stocks in a day. One minute, a stock's price increase. Thefollowing minute, the same stock's price crashes because no one decided to buy it. Aside from the demand, other factors may have affected the rise and fall of a stock's price such as the financial condition of the issuing company, political and governmental situation and inflation.

The point, do not invest your money in stocks if you do not know what you are dealing with. Ignorance can bring you massive losses.

Inflation risk

Inflation risk refers to the decrease in purchasing power an investor has. You can't buy the same item at the same price and the same quantity as compared years ago. For example, you could buy 10 candies with a dollar five years ago. Today, you can still buy the same brand of candies with a dollar but the quantity decreases. Perhaps today, you can only buy 5 or lesser.

How does this risk affect your stock investing approach? Suppose, you buy a stock that yields 4% payout and you invest the rest of your money in the bank that earns 4% interest. In effect, you are earning. Your first investment might be at risk with the increases in interest rate and financial condition of the issuing company. Your second investment is safe and is not at risk with a higher interest rate. Since you have invested the rest in a bank, your money earns whatever interest that the bank uses.

However, the inflation rate is around 5%. Your earnings are below the inflation rate. This means your investment in the bank is losing money.

Tax Risk

Tax risk is the decrease in what you can get. The purpose of stock investing is to build wealth. When there is wealth, a tax is present. You need to pay a portion for tax obligations. This means you have to be knowledgeable on tax so that you can avoid paying more taxes than you earn.

Political Risk

Sometimes, when the government issues new rules and regulations, some companies are affected. Others may even become bankrupt because of a particular law while some companies may profit from this same law. In a toxic and unfair political environment, companies may die or live. Thus, it does not hurt if you have a basic knowledge of how politics work in countries because political and governmental conflicts can affect a company's financial condition. In some countries, companies might become political targets.

Personal and Emotional Risk

Personal risk refers to your incapacity to increase your investment when an opportunity arises. This may also refer to your inability to maintain an investment because you need cash immediately. The first scenario arises when you have enough money to invest but are afraid to buy more. Alternatively, it could be that you do not have the money because you have spent it in an emergency. The second scenario arises when you do not have an emergency fund to pay for your emergencies. The first thing you need to do is ensuring that you have an emergency fund when you begin stock investing. If you skip that step, you are more likely to experience these scenarios sooner or .

Emotional risk refers to your inability to control emotions when you decide to buy or sell a stock investment. Most of the times, many investors let their emotions control their rational thinking. In stock investing, you are either greedy for more or be afraid to lose money. These are extreme emotions that you should learn to control when investing in stocks.

How to Manage Risk

Stock market investing may involve so many risks but minimizing such risks is easy and attainable. Don't let these risks hinder you from investing. Risks should not be your major criterion in deciding whether to invest or not.

Stop, Gather and Learn

Before investing your money in stocks, gather as much information as you can manage. Learn everything you need to know about stocks investing. The more information you know the greater is your chance in making and choosing winning stocks. If it takes you years to understand even the basic language of stock investing, so be it.

The important thing is minimizing risks of losing money into a venture you know nothing about. Indeed, you might argue that the best teacher is experience, but it does not mean you have to face a battle without preparing for it. If you think you are not ready, then don't start buying stocks even with the insistence of a financial adviser. Financial advisers may be experts in their field but they are not the ones who will suffer the loss.

Remember the Basics

Whenever you feel strong enough to fight, always remember the basics. Make sure to keep yourself grounded and always go back to the basics of stock investing. These basic concepts can help you reach your goals without losing a large amount of money.

Diversification

This refers to a mix-and-match approach in stock investing. You don't concentrate on one investment. Your portfolio consists of short-term, intermediate and long-term investments. The percentage depends on your personal style of investment. If you are an aggressive investor, the majority of your investment money is placed on short-term and intermediate investments. A lesser percentage is on long-term investment. If you are a conservative investor, most likely, a huge chunk of your investment money is placed on long-term investment. Only a small percentage is on short-term and intermediate.

Another way of diversifying is by investing your money in different financial instruments. Do not concentrate your investment money on stocks alone since the stock market is a volatile market.

14. Understanding Strike Price

A strike price is a fixed price at which an options contract can be exercised. The term is mainly used when describing index and stock options.

How strike price works

The options contract has specified stripe prices. In put options, the value of the underlying asset while trading is referred to as the strike price. In call options, the holder earns the right to buy an underlying asset at the set strike price up to the expiry date. In put options, it is the price the underlying asset is traded by an option buyer up to the expiry date. In the call option, the strike price refers to the amount an investor buys the underlying asset up to the expiry date. The strike price is also referred to as the exercise price. It is an essential factor in establishing the value of an option.

Importance of Strike Price

While pricing options, this is the most crucial factor to consider. While exercising an option, the profit earned is determined by the difference between the stock's market price and the option strike price at the expiration date. A strike price can help you establish if an investment is worth your time or not. You can come out with a loss or a profit depending on the strike price involved. As an investor, you want to know the investments that bring high returns and avoid those that will result in a loss. Knowing the strike price can help you deciding on which trades to make. You also get to avoid the trades that could result in losing your investment.

The concept of Moneyness

Moneyness refers to the quality of a financial contract. This occurs if the contract settlement is financial. It can be established by obtaining the difference between the strike price and the current trade price for an underlying asset.

Terms like out-of-the-money, in-the-money, and at-the-money can be used to explain the moneyness of options in trading.

Intrinsic Value

The intrinsic value can also be referred to as the monetary value of an asset. It is the quality of an underlying asset if it is exercised immediately. A call can get a positive intrinsic value if the stock price of the underlying asset is higher than the set price, which is the strike price. This is what we refer to as in-the-money. Out-of-the-money occurs when a put option has no value.

Time Value

This refers to the value of an option, excluding the intrinsic value. It occurs when it is difficult to establish the future price movements of an asset. Knowing the time value can aid in establishing the possible discounts that are in an option between when it was bought and when it expires. The time value is negative when it comes to European options. This is influenced by the fact that the option cannot be exercised until it gets to the expiration date.

Why should you care about how options are priced

As an investor, it is very crucial to know how various options are priced. Knowing the prices saves one from the possibility of being overpriced or under priced depending on the situation at hand. While evaluating the prices, you also get to identify the possible investments that you can engage in depending on your budget. This, alongside other reasons, shows the importance of knowing how options are priced.

1. It allows you to know what to invest in.

As a beginner, you may be stranded and unable to identify the best investment that you can engage in. Before engaging in a trade, it is always good to conduct a proper evaluation. This analysis helps you know all that is required if you before engaging in business. Understanding the prices helps you know that which you can afford to invest in. You will find that some options demand that you spend a vast some money. While at it, you will identify some that need little investments.

The one that demands that you part with a small portion of your finances may appear to be very appealing. You will find that most amateur trades will prefer beginning with such. After all, you get to the part with a small piece of your income and generate profits. You forget to put all other factors into consideration, such as option strategies and end up focusing on the price. Higher chances are that you are likely to encounter a massive loss in the trade since you know very little about what you are engaging in. This is why you should consider the pricing before engaging in any form of commerce.

While getting a brokerage account, you need to be very careful with the features and services provided by the account. By evaluating the option pricing, you will identify accounts that have peculiar pricing, and this should raise the alarm. The pricing that does not rhyme with the rest should help you know the official brokerage accounts and those that are not genuine. As the options trading markets expand, we have a lot of competition being created. This results in the creations on multiple accounts of which, some are a pure scam. Knowing the options pricing will help you identify the excellent option trading accounts.

In some cases, you may find some trades that have high pricing. You also find that the returns are equally good, and it appears like an excellent investment to make. When you decide to engage in it, you may end up getting a considerable profit. If at all, you had no information about the option and especially the pricing, it would be challenging to execute it. The fact that you have knowledge of the pricing helps you identify it as a good investment, and you decide to engage in the trade.

2. You can identify the best option strategy to use.

You find that each procedure is different in its ways, and the pricing varies. Knowing option pricing will help you identify the best strategy to utilize in every situation. While analyzing the various Options strategies, you may discover that some are more profitable than others. In some cases, one may not get any profit and remain at a stagnant point without making returns. This information becomes useful in that it guides you in investing in the right strategy.

3. You can minimize risks

It is expected that the investment in options trading comes with its risks. There are a number of challenges that you will encounter. On the bright side, some of these downsides can be predicted. Due to this factor, it becomes easy to manage them and make the right trade. If you can look into option pricing, managing some of these risks becomes easy. You can evaluate the option pricing and get to know the trades that are not profitable. Imagine the amount of trouble you will have saved yourself from if you knew how the options are priced.

4. There is room for increasing return

The dream of every investor is to get the highest possible profits. You want to see yourself running a profitable business that will unbelievably transform your income generation ability. This does not only have to be a dream, but you can make it happen. Knowing how options are priced enables you to establish the options that are profitable. Trading in such opportunities will help you earn high returns and make your dreams a reality.

5. It helps in choosing a cost-effective option

We are regularly advised to live within our means. I am a believer that people should also trade within their means. While deciding on the best option to invest in, try to aim at choosing a cost-effective strategy. By doing so, you will be able to trade in that which you can afford. If things go contrary to what you anticipated, you will get a loss, but it will not be as bad as if never invested in what you can afford to lose. The option prices play a significant role in having a cost-effective option.

From the above reasons provided, it is clear why you need to be concerned about how options are priced. The option pricing has a significant influence on options trading. It helps you identify the best options to engage in. If you have a vision of becoming an expert in options trading, you should be able to take a close look into the option pricing. You will identify the options that can result in a loss and those that are profitable and worth investing your income on. To make a fortune out of your investment, consider taking a keen look at how options are priced.

15. Get Rid of the Bad Behavior

Some of the worst things that new or intermediate investors can do is to look at successful investors who model bad habits. We will go through some of these habits below in hopes that they can be modified or avoided completely to ensure you have greater success than those who engage in them. Having a healthy mindset creates stability and also helps to drive well-informed decisions that are not based on emotions. Basically, there is no room for emotions in a financial numbers market. Here is a list of what to do/not do.

Do not start off by sticking to one particular stock.

You need to cast off the emotions of being tied to a certain stock. The best investors may do well for a long while, and accrue considerable wealth, but every stock has its end, and the best investors also know when it is time to cash out. Emotionally, it is hard for some people to let go of the thought that a stock is something to ride out through thick and thin.

This is generally a good framework, and it keeps you from short-term sales, but even when a stock does well it also has its glory days and they will fade so get out while it is good. By selling your favorite stocks you can also think of it as investing the assets you have gained into something else. Nothing lasts forever, so you need to move and be flexible. Some people may choose to stay with a losing stock on the other hand. That is entirely a different factor!

You also want to avoid selling stocks when it is not the right time. This will be covered more, . Selling either too soon or too late are other problems. Many people do this based on emotion as well, and not necessarily based on their actual performance.

Do not try to chase the stock if it loses

Some investors are gluttons for punishment and cannot accept the fact that a particular stock is a losing stock. They may try to chase the loss by coming back at a time to repurchase the same company's stock. Some think of this as "I'll show you" type thinking; a semblance of punishment to the stock itself that demonstrates to the investor that they can and will beat the market this time.

Irrational thinking is a huge barrier to success in the market and it will catch up to you every time. Some call it mythological thinking. People have fantasy notions, distorted beliefs about why a stock works or did not work. None or little of that may be true. Allow the numbers and histories of the stock speak to you. As a beginner, you learned how to read and analyze stocks. Sometimes a refresher is needed, to stay objective and to avoid this fantasy thinking.

Do not hold onto dead weight.

Although a good rule of thumb is to forget anything you have sold there are times when you may want to revisit an old stock. If you are in a position where you are holding dead stock you will only see its value spin downwards and it will not come back up most likely, so selling it would be a good choice. However, some investors think that losses are due to bad timing and luck.

Some people delude themselves into thinking until they sell their failed stock they haven't really lost anything, and besides, it may return!! If it comes back then mentally it may seem that it was a wash, or a win. This is also irrational thinking. Additionally, wishing, hoping, thinking and praying that a stock revive itself will not make it a reality.

If a stock you finally sold off had lost but then bounces back, forget it unless it has completely recovered and is super strong.

Not all stocks bounce back. Most of the major company's stocks that are reflected in stock market charts show a comeback that is evident in graphs. Smaller or lesser known companies do not always follow these trajectories and they may bottom out. This is often overlooked as well. The big guys tend to follow different patterns.

16. Trading and Time

When one thinks of the different investment tools, if not the practice, of the investment in general, one cannot but considers the temporal factor. This is one of the factors that other miller discourages the trader. But why?

In these times, we are so used to the concept of everything and immediately we cannot wait any longer. We demand everything immediately, also losing track of time and the precious value of time.

Unfortunately, in online trading, you cannot expect to have everything and immediately, but above all, we cannot expect to become experienced traders and professionals in just under a month or worse than a week.

You cannot think of becoming an expert trader if you do not want to study and practice! In online trading, but also in investment, in general, it takes time to learn how to trade. Another advice that is not feasible at the moment is to think about spending some time to find a deserving, professional, and worthy investment and investment technique.

When trading, it must be done seriously and professionally. If, for example, we trade in a trading strategy based on currency trading, with a maximum payout of 65% for a positively closed trade, then we must enter the perspective that we must give money to work with a specific strategy.

If you are following the market trend, it will be counterproductive to exit the market because, in addition to losing its capital, you may not even get the desired return. That's why time is money, and it should not be wasted unnecessarily. Above all, hurry is a bad companion.

The time factor is also one of the main factors for which it is decided better to entrust its capital to a financial expert so that this is to make the choices for them. Very often, however, this trust is not always repaid by an increase in one's capital. Most often this capital is completely lost.

The Importance Of The Right Time And Timing

Understanding when the right time to trade is very important. Giving money to mature is certainly one of the most determining factors for the success of your investment. The fundamental concept remains the same: within what you want to earn money and how to earn them.

To make sure that you know, in advance, how much you can earn and how to make money for us, you cannot rely on chance, and above all, we cannot expect to waste time but not even to demand everything immediately.

Everything has its time; also, in investment, they have their right times and their importance. As you can see, even the right timing serves to give way to the investment, to make your own cycle, and to express that reasonable expectation. The right setup also serves your capital to survive in any situation, resist negative moments, and always have the strength to start again.

Avoiding Risks

To better understand the risks involved in trading in risky strategies, it seems right to remember those that are the right principles. Suppose you can trade $10,000 in a strategy that is 50% risk. This strategy was put in place to double the capital within a maximum of 3. Highly risky strategy from our point of view as it could result in the total loss of the entire capital. This operation is recommended only to experienced traders.

With this example, we have made you understand how these operations allow you to double or triple the capital within a few months but also how you can lose all your capital in a matter of months. In fact, by implementing these dangerous strategies, you will also see the account halved, or entirely burned, within a few weeks.

To understand everything better, let's take another example. According to your trading strategies, you have traded on a particular asset with a strategy and think that this can give you a return of 50% within a month.

To not fall into error, we advise you to set the opposite goal or try to ask the question: how would it be if in half a month you lost half of the bill? Here is therefore explained and understood in a simple and fast way on what is the right time, but especially those that are the wrong strategies not to be adopted.

Limiting Damages of Social Trading

Many wonders if social trading is the right strategy to avoid wasting time and earning, thanks to social trading. Before proceeding, we remind you that social trading is not a risk-free form of trading, even if the risk, in this case, is reduced. To trade in social trading, we believe it is essential to operate for a period of time between 9 and 12 months minimum. This is for one simple reason. Before choosing an investment system, you must see the performance for at least a year. In this sense, there is no need to follow a trader, 24 hours a day, 365 days a year, but only that you have to consult all the data of all the operations performed during the year, perhaps with the help with special tools that simplify reading.

Once you understand how to trade, but above all, you understand how much trading and who you want to trade in, you have to consider the risk that you are willing to run. Beyond this limit, it is advisable to leave it alone.

In most cases, the conditions that have led you to make a certain investment choice must have solid foundations so that the investment can yield. That's why a period of 12 months is a period enough to make you understand if your investment is right or wrong.

17. Price Charts

There are three kinds of price charts you will encounter in the markets. The first is the one which provides the least amount of information and is generally used by popular media like TV channels and so on. Perhaps there's a connection there, but anyway, this chart is the simple line chart which depicts price as a line, going up or down with the percent change following to it in either red or green.

Plotting this line is simple enough. You place a dot for the level at which price closed the former day and connect it to the dot which symbolizes market close or current price at a given moment, and you have a line which is either above, below, or at the same level. This is what the percent change measures. The line chart looks pretty and provides easy conclusions for non-specialists and as such, you will not find any trader ever looking at price represented this way.

The following kind of chart, which is a huge improvement over the humble line chart, is the American bar chart. I'm calling this American because it is usually found only Stateside and not so much around the world. The representation of price in a bar chart is shown in Figure 1 below.

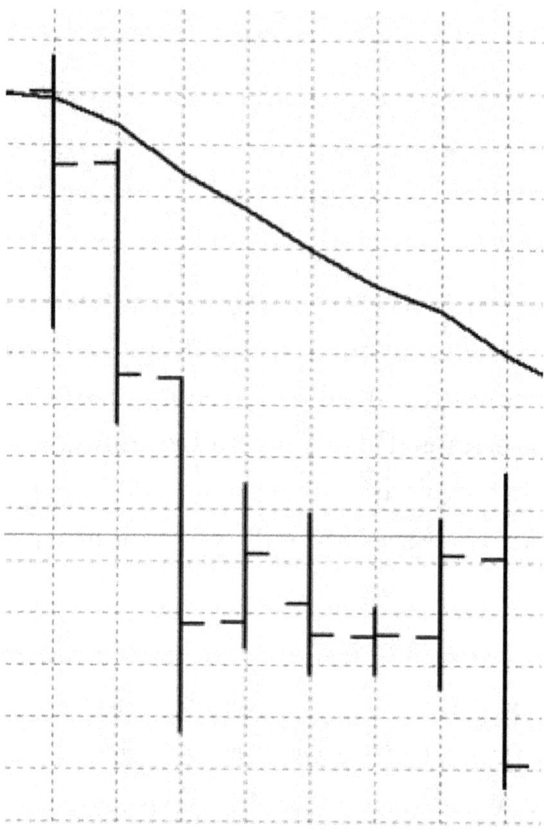

Figure 1: A bar chart (MetaTrader 4, 2015)

Each bar in this image represents price action for a given interval. So, if these bars were on a daily chart, one bar represents what price did during that entire day. If it's a sixty-minute chart, it represents hourly price action and so on. Let's break this down more.

The vertical line represents the range of price movement. Thus, the top of this line is the high that price achieved during this interval and the lowest point is the low during the same interval. The larger the vertical line is, the greater the range with which price moved. The notch on either side of the vertical line signifies the open and close, with the open on the left and close on the right.

Bars are fantastic this way because they don't need any special color or design characteristics. By just looking at the notches, we can see whether price increased during the interval or decreased. If the notch on the right is higher than the one on the left, then the price increased, and if the one on the left is higher, then the price decreased during the time interval.

The relative positions of the open and close notches to the high and low provide excellent information with regards to the price action during the session. For example, a close that's far above the low and the high, that is with a tail, signifies buying pressure that overcame selling pressure. The same applies if a wick exists to the top.

Bars, despite the amount of information they provide, do have their shortcomings. For one, they're not the most graphically communicative. When seen in a cluster, the bars do tend to blend in with one another. The most informative way of communicating price action is "candlesticks" and this is what most professional traders use.

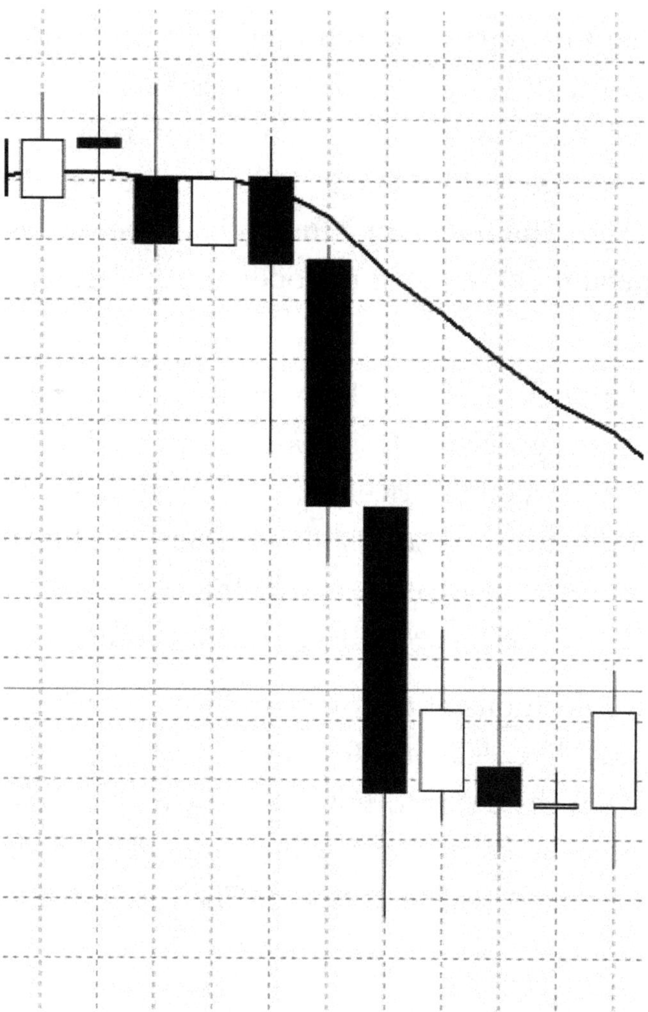

Figure 2: Candlestick chart

Candlesticks, or candles as they're called, have the same information as bars do. They communicate the open, close, high low, and the range within which price moved during the given time interval. The difference is that the body of the candle is a far more graphic representation of the range. Aside from communicating the extent of the price range, the color of the bar informs us whether price decreased or increased during the time interval.

Bullish bars or bars whose close is higher than the open, have a different color from bearish ones, that is bars where the close is below the open. The colors can be chosen by the trader and conventionally, charting platforms assign the color red to bearish bars and blue to bullish ones.

Candlesticks provide an instant snapshot of price action and they can be traded individually via patterns. The highs and the lows are represented by the wicks on either side of the body and the size of the body, wick size, and location with respect to the candle body form a pattern which can be used to draw conclusions.

Let's look at a few patterns that will help you get up and running quickly.

Candlestick Patterns

The first pattern that will prove extremely useful to you is the inside bar. This is shown in figure 3.

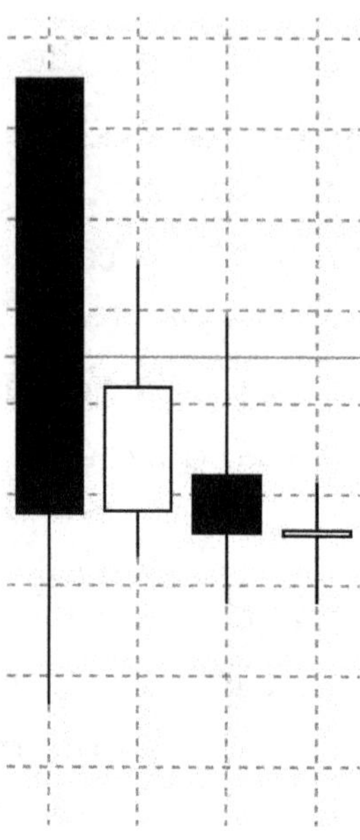

Figure 3: Inside bar cluster (MetaTrader 4, 2015)

The pattern is comprised of two bars, with the one on the right lying within the range of the body of the bar on the left. Now, it isn't fully necessary for the smaller bar's wicks to be completely within the bigger bar's body. It's far more important that the order flow characteristics of this pattern is understood.

Inside bars are a continuation pattern which indicates that the current market situation will persist. Thus, if the market is in a bull trend and then price hesitates sideways and forms an inside bar, you can bet that the original trend will continue. This is true of bullish and bearish trends.

The only market situation where you should not be trading is when inside bars are in ranges. If you're not familiar with what trends and ranges However, for now, just remember that inside bars, and indeed all price patterns, are meant to be used in certain environments.

The following useful candlestick pattern is the pin bar which is illustrated in figure 4.

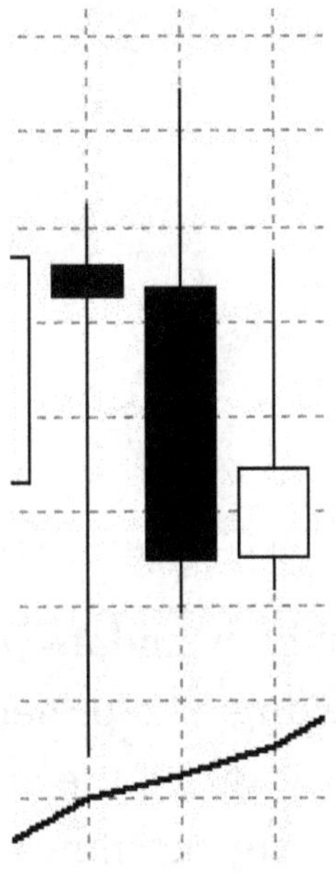

Figure 4: Pin bars on either side of a bearish bar (MetaTrader 4, 2015)

The pin bar is a single bar formation and signifies a reversal. Despite being a reversal pattern, the best way to trade this for a beginner is to do so with trend. This means that when price moves in a small sideways pattern once it takes a breather in a trend, look out for a pin bar to signify the end of the sideways pattern and resumption of the trend. Figure 5 illustrates how this works.

Figure 5: Pin bar provides continuation signal (MetaTrader 4, 2015)

The pin bar is characterized by a small body and a wick or tail above or below the body. Generally speaking, it is preferable to have the wick or tail's length to be at least thrice the size of the body. Again, don't get caught up in measuring things, just understand the underlying trade mechanics.

Wicks and tails happen when traders reject a certain price level strongly. This is even more significant if the body is small because it indicates that the original downward or upward movement was strong but then it was rejected by an even stronger movement that produces the wick or the tail. When such a pattern occurs at or near an important support or resistance level, it is about as blaring a sign the market will ever give you as to which direction it is about to move in.

"Support and Resistance" is discussed in detail in a separate but in case you're unfamiliar with these, they're essentially important order flow levels where traders draw lines in the sand and defend it. S/R is an important skill set for you to master in order to trade successfully.

The last candlestick pattern that will prove itself extremely useful is the climaxing pattern. The climax occurs at the very end of a bullish or bearish move and is accompanied by what can be best termed as "exaggerations". The sizes of the bars involved are exaggerated far beyond the usual size in the trend; the volumes peak massively and the rebound of the climax is fast and sharp as well.

Climaxes are counter-trend trades and generally, I don't recommend beginners trade in this manner but it is actually a simple trade to take once you learn how to spot a climax. The reason it is simple is because you don't need to worry about S/R or any other market events.

Figure 6: Bear trend ends in a climax

Climaxes are also referred to as exhaustive movements and are characterized by massive trend bars accompanied by huge volumes. The bar sizes and volumes are not just larger than ordinary but far larger, almost twice the magnitude. It is important that you look for this extreme exaggeration since it indicates that weak with trend players, in other words--the uninformed public, has entered the market and are jumping onto the bandwagon right when it's too late.

What follows as climax is either a sideways movement which eventually leads to a trend reversal or a sharp counter-trend bounce that is then followed by a meandering sideways movement. This is advantageous and we'll see how to trade these sideways movements when talking about ranges .

Climaxes are excellent in terms of the ROI they offer on your time as well. Given the pace with which price moves counter-trend post the climax, you'll earn your profits soon. From a rice environment perspective, you want to look for these near the end of trends and not in ranges. Climaxes give birth to ranges and don't occur within them.

This covers the main points in terms of the market basics you need to know and understand. The key lesson to take away from all this is that the market is just a giant collection of orders being matched with one another and that these orders reflect sentiment.

Sentiment is not always logical but is always chaotic. However, over a long enough period, sentiment leaves patterns which repeat themselves more often than not. By ensuring we can spot such patterns and recognize the odds inherent in them, we can trade successfully.

For now, remember that you don't necessarily need indicators or special tools to trade the market. Indicators are simply derived from price and as such, the price chart has all the information you need. Traders tend to rely on indicators because the seeming complexity of the price chart scares them.

Options take away a lot of this problem but before we dive into options' basics, it is important to get to know that most important person in your trading business--your broker. In addition, you will also need to learn about the laws surrounding trading and why it is important to be well-capitalized.

18. Options Greeks

Now that we know what influences the prices of options, we are going to make that more quantifiable. This is done using the so-called "Greeks," which are five parameters denoted by Greek symbols (or letters) that quantify the way the price of an option will change. You don't have to know how they work precisely, only what they mean. At any given time, you can look them up to get their values. We start by looking at intrinsic value, that is, how the price of the option changes or varies with the underlying stock's price.

Delta

If you look at the data for any option, you are going to see five Greek letters (usually expressed by their English spelled names) delta, theta, gamma, vega, and rho. The first of these is delta, which tells you how the price of an option changes with the price of the underlying stock.

We noted earlier that the price of an option doesn't have a 1-1 change in price in relation to the stock. You can see exactly how it will change by looking at delta. First, we'll consider call options. So if delta is 0.46, that means if the underlying stock price rises by $1, the price of the option is going to increase by $0.46. If delta were 0.74, then the price of the option would rise by $0.74 if the price of the underlying stock went up by $1.

Put options have a negative delta, which just indicates that a put option has an inverse relationship to the price of the underlying stock. That is if the price of the underlying stock goes down, the value of a put option goes up, and if the price of the underlying stock goes up, the value of the put option goes down.

So if delta is -0.26, and the price of the underlying stock went up by $1, the value of the put option would drop by 26 cents. On the other hand, if the price of the underlying stock had dropped by $1, then the price of the put option would rise by $0.26.

Delta is dynamic, and the number always changes when some important parameter in the options price changes. Consider an option on a stock that is trading at $102 with a strike price of $100, with 14 days to option expiration. In this case, the price of the call option is $2.48, and delta is 0.75. The price of the put option is $0.47, and delta for the put option is -0.25. So if the price of the underlying stock goes up by $1, we expect the call option to rise to $2.48 + $0.75 = $3.23. The price of the put option would decrease to $0.47 - $0.25 = $0.22.

That's just about what happens, but in reality, the relationship isn't quite exact since other things impact the price of the options. The call option increases to $3.84, and the put option declines in price to $0.27.

We said its dynamic, and what happens when the share price rises by $1, is the delta values for both options change as well. Now delta is 0.84 for the call, and -0.16 for the put.

That tells us something important, namely that delta is higher the more in the money the stock is. We can see this looking at some real options. Considering an IBM $124 call that expires on 6/28, it has a delta of 0.967. A $139 call that expires on 6/28 has a delta of 0.5388. The share price is $139.20, so the $124 call is more in the money. The $139 call is practically at the money, and we learn a second important fact about delta, that is that at the money options will have a delta that is reasonably close to 0.50.

Since the more in the money you are, the higher delta, that means in the money options can benefit (or be hurt by) a $1 change in the price of the underlying stock.

Something else that happens is that if the option is in the money, the closer you get to expiration, the higher delta goes. For our example of an option with a $100 share price, if the underlying stock price remains at $103, moving to 7 days from expiration, delta jumps to 0.92 for the call. Moving to 3 days to expiration, delta is 0.98. So if you are expecting a stock price to move a lot in the following few days, getting an option that will expire soon before the move happens could be a worthwhile investment. Look for events that could impact the price, such as an earnings call or product announcement.

Remember at the money options have a delta of about 0.50, and when you get close to expiration, delta for a call will be exactly 0.50, and for a put, it will be -0.5, if the option was at the money. Actually buying at the money options can be quite difficult, so you'll probably have to settle for something close.

If an option is out of the money, the closer to the expiration date, you get the smaller delta gets. In fact, a few days away from expiration delta can get ravishingly small. An out of the money call option for a strike price of $100, share price of $97 with three days to expiration will have a delta of 0.02.

The delta for the same put option will add up the difference to 100 (but remember it's expressed as a negative value). In this case, a put option with the same parameters, so a strike price of $100 – will have a delta of -0.98 if the underlying price is $97. In that case, the put would be worth $3.00, and if the underlying share price dropped to $96, the price of the put would rise to $4. Then you'd see delta increase to -1.00 for the put and drop to 0.00 for the call.

If the stock had moved the other way, risen in price by $1, then delta for the put would drop to -0.92 instead, and the price of the put would drop to $2.04.

The bottom line is delta will give you a good estimate of how much the price of the option will change when the price of the underlying stock changes by $1. If it's a call option, the relationship is direct, and delta is expressed as a positive number. For put options, since the relationship is an inverse one, delta is a negative number. And remember that if you take the absolute value of delta for the put option and add it to the delta value for a call option that has the same strike value and date of expiration, they will sum to 1.0.

Gamma

Gamma is like the second derivative. In other words, it tells you how delta itself changes. This is important since we noted that delta was dynamic. However, beginning traders don't need to dive into this too deeply, but you can check gamma to see about how much delta will change if there is a $1 change in the price of the underlying shares. Gamma has the same value for both puts and calls. So if Gamma were 0.22 and delta was 0.24 for a call option, and -0.76 for a put option with the same strike and expiration date, we'd expect a $1 rise in share price to cause delta for the call option to increase to 0.46, and the delta for the put option would change to -0.54. That is about what would happen, but remember if the option were at the money the values of delta would move to 0.5 and -0.5, respectively.

Theta

When examining options, theta is a very important parameter among the Greeks. What theta gives you information about is the time decay of the option. Theta is expressed as a negative number, reflecting the fact that time decay causes a decrease in option price as time goes on.

Let's consider a couple of examples.

Suppose that we have call and put options with a strike price of $100 with three days to expiration. The price of the call is $1.20, and the price of the put is $0.20 if the share price of the underlying stock is $101. In this case, theta is -0.073 for both the call and the put. That tells us that if nothing else changes, the price of each option will decrease by $0.073. The call option is priced at $1.20, and the put is priced at $0.20. Moving to 2 days to expiration and leaving everything else the same, we find that the price of the call option drops to $1.12, and the price of the put option drops to $0.12, so it moved in almost exact accordance to what was expected. The following day theta has increased to -0.079, reflecting the fact that time decay happens more rapidly the closer you get to the expiration date of the option.

In fact, with everything else unchanged, 20 days to expiration theta is about half as strong, at -0.035. That reflects one of the fundamental truths of options, that is that time decay happens in an exponential fashion, with time decay happening faster the closer you get to expiration.

One of the things that help make options seem complicated is that all of these variables are interdependent. So at 20 days to expiration, suppose the stock price shot up to $108. In that case, theta decreases to -0.005. So it's only 1/7th of the former value. It decreases for the put option as well.

Theta is also proportional to share price. So theta is larger if the share price is larger. Consider a stock with a share price of $975, and a strike price of $1,000. In that case, theta is -0.282 for the call option and -0.274 for the put option. That means if a day passes and nothing else changes, the value of the call option (which in this case is $5.15) will drop by about $0.28, and the value of the put option will drop by about $0.27.

The fundamental lesson here is the same as it was formerly, that time decay is an important fundamental when it comes to options pricing. Check the Greek theta to get an idea of how the price of the option is going to decay by the following day if all other things are held equal.

19. Investigating ROI from Trading Options

As alternative brokers, we should pick between contending open doors for utilizing our limited exchanging reserves. Some portion of the determination procedure needs to include computing the conceivable quantifiable profit. This is somewhat more trying for alternative exchanges than it would be for single-dimensional instruments like stocks or fates, since options costs don't pursue stock costs in a straight manner. All things considered; with the correct devices we can focus in on the measurements we need.

We accept (suppose) that the in all likelihood way at the cost of the stock US Steel (X) is to switch out of the stockpile zone it is as of now in at around $38.00, and head down to the last significant interest zone around $32.00. This excursion took around six exchanging days last time it happened in March 2017 (not appeared on the outline); however, we'll enable a month to be sheltered.

The time frame is significant on the grounds that the costs of alternatives gradually go down after some time through the procedure called time rot. That is a headwind that we need to consider.

What we have to decide is:

In the first place, how about we think about how we would make these estimations if we somehow happened to exchange not simply the options, however the stock. We'll utilize a 100-share parcel to make figuring straightforward. Here is the thing that the arrangement would be:

Undercut 100 portions of the stock when/in the event that it drops down through the proximal (lower) line of our interest zone at 37.00. This development would be the affirmation that the normal inversion has started.

Or on the other hand drop the exchange without entering it if X transcends the distal (upper) line of the interest zone at 38.41 before dipping under 37.00. All things considered, our stock zone would have been demonstrated not sufficiently able to turn around the bearing and we would search for another chance. No damage, no foul.

Once in the exchange, take benefit by purchasing to cover the short position if/when the cost of X drops to our objective at 31.99.

Then again, if after we enter the exchange and the cost of X transcends our upper limit at 38.41, we will leave the exchange for a little misfortune. We'll permit somewhat of a cradle if there should be an occurrence of a little trip over the line, suppose $10. Along these lines, we'll purchase to cover the position if the cost of X transcends 38.51.

Here is the manner by which this exchange spreads out (all figures are per share):

- ➤ Section Price $37.00

- ➤ Stop-misfortune Price $38.51

- ➤ Misfortune whenever halted out $ 1.49 ($149 aggregate on 100 offers)

- ➤ Passage Price $37.00

- ➤ Target Price $31.99

- ➤ Increase whenever shut at objective $ 5.01 ($501 aggregate on 100 offers)

- ➤ Reward: Risk Ratio ($5.01/$1.49) 3.36: 1

- ➤ Rate of profitability ($5.01/$37.00) 13.54%

Along these lines, the proposed exchange offers a reward to chance proportion of more than 3 to 1, and an arrival on speculation of 13.54% if effective.

Presently, how about we consider this exchange if utilizing alternatives rather than offers. To begin with, how about we expect that as opposed to undercutting 100 portions of stock, we got one Put options at the following strike cost simply over our stockpile zone, which is the $39.00 strike. Each put alternative speaks to 100 portions of stock. We'll utilize a put that terminates a while out, say in April 2018.

The April $39.00 Put could be purchased for $403 as of now. This put alternative in fact gives us the privilege to sell 100 portions of X stock at $39.00 per share, whenever among now and the end of business on April 18, 2018. We really have no aim of practicing this option (all things considered, we have no portions of X to sell). Realizing that the estimation of put alternatives goes up when the cost of the stock goes down, we will likely sell the put itself at a more significant expense than the $400 we paid for it. It isn't important to possess any portions of the stock on which you purchase options.

When the cost of X dropped to our $31.99 focus, for instance, the put would be worth at any rate the distinction between $3199 (the expense at which one could purchase 100 offers on the open market around then), and $3900 (the cost at which the $39 put gives us the ensured appropriate to sell the offers around then). This distinction would be $3900 − $3199, or $701 least estimation of the put with the stock at our objective. Truth be told, the put would be worth more than that

$701 least (which is called its natural worth), contingent upon how much time was left in the put's life when we wished to sell it. The more it needed to go, the more alleged time esteem it would have, notwithstanding the $701 of characteristic worth.

Yet, first of all, suppose it was the very day of lapse when the cost of X came to our $31.99 target. All things considered, there would be no time esteem (no time left) and the put would be worth $701. Given that we paid $403 for the put initially, we would have a benefit of $701 − $403 = $302. On a $403 venture, this is a pace of return of $302/$403 or 75%.

In the event that our objective was hit sooner than the termination day, at that point, the put would hold additional time worth, and we could sell it at a greater expense and benefit. For instance, if the objective was hit in a month, the estimation of the put is anticipated to be $755. This projection is finished utilizing an alternative P/L chart, which is a standard element of most options exchanging stages. I will portray the utilization of that apparatus in future articles.

Utilizing that equivalent P/L diagram apparatus, we can extend that if as opposed to dropping to our objective, X hits our stop-misfortune cost of $38.51 every month from now, the estimation of the put around then would be $337. In the event that that happened, we would sell the put at that $337 cost and assume our moderately little misfortune.

We presently have what we have to look at the two exchanges:

- Short Stock April $39 Put

- Passage Price $37.00 per share $403

- Stop-misfortune Price $38.51 $337

- Misfortune whenever halted out $ 1.49 ($ 149 aggregate on 100 offers) $ 66

- Section Price $37.00 per share $403

- Target Price $38.51 $753

- Addition whenever shut at objective $ 5.01 ($501 aggregate on 100 offers) $350

- Reward: Risk Ratio 3.36: 1 ($5.01/$1.49) 5.3: 1 ($350/$66)

- Degree of profitability 13.54% ($5.01/37.00) 86.8% ($350/$403)

20. Options Trading Advantages and Lingo

During personal financial management, an investment strategy for you to consider is options trading. However, before indulging in this strategy, you will need to understand the various guidelines, advice, terminologies and influencing factors outlined here. Only once have you fully understood this base knowledge, can you consider getting started in options trading.

Should You Or Should You Not Work With Options?

You need to identify the backbone of options trading to maximize the benefits and minimize or eliminate its downside. You must adhere to the following three strategic elements when you are considering the potential benefits or negatives of investing in options:

You need to determine the likely direction of your stock movement

The directionality of your stock price movement determines which type of option to buy. When trading in options, you buy contracts, which will then allow you to trade options as specified by your standard of commitment. There are two types of options contracts: call options and put options.

A call option will make you money in a market where stock prices are trending upwards. Put contracts are the exact opposite; you will make money when the prices go down. Remember, to buy the appropriate type of option, first; you will need to determine the potential direction of stock price movement during a specified period. Here is an example; if you think the stock price is bound to rise over the given period, you should buy a call option.

If the stock price goes up as you speculated, then you stand to make money since the value of the stock will have increased from your initial strike price. Now, buying a put option becomes worthwhile when the stock price falls per your initial downward trend prediction. You only make a profit when the stock prices move in a direction following your initial speculation. Hence, your thinking in the course of stock movement will determine which type of options for you to trade.

You need to predict your maximum or minimum stock value limits within specific periods

This information is crucial in determining the price at which you may need to purchase or sell a particular option contract. This buying or selling price of your options contract is the strike price. For instance, you determine that the value of a specific stock will never go above X dollars over a specified period. Therefore, you will buy that call option at a strike price that is less than X dollars. After the expiry period, this move guarantees that your call option remains profitable if your former assumption holds.

In the case of put options, we recommend the opposite trading moves on your part. You expect that the stock price will trend downwards over the specified period. You predict that the stock price will never fall below Y dollars. Hence, you will need to buy relevant put contracts at a higher strike price. At the end of the expiry period, your put option likewise remains profitable. Hence, knowing how particular stocks trend and their history are vital to predicting the potential limits of their valuation over time.

Options brokers know this information since they have experience dealing with various stock types and understand their market trends. When you tap into this knowledge, you will end up making informed decisions on when to enter or exit a particular trade. In long term trading, an inspired strike price will result in huge returns on your initial investments over time.

You need to estimate the time frame within which your stock movements will take place

Your options trade contract will have an expiry duration beyond which your option cannot trade. When dealing in the options market, your trading restricts within the period specified in your particular options contract. It is essential to exercise your appropriate trade moves during this period and especially at a time when the deal seems profitable.

This opportunity typically arises when the stock movement matches your expected trend. When you wait too long, the market trends will start moving in the opposite direction to your preference, and you may start losing money. The length of your contract duration also plays a factor in determining the profitability of your trading options. These duration are often predetermined depending on the type of choice you trade. However, you can choose the preferred nature of the length of your investment.

Based on this nature, your investment may be either long term or short term. Short-term duration typically last days or weeks while long-term investments stretch over months, fiscal quarters or even years. For your information, here are some reasons why long-term investments are preferable. Your trading in options over long periods will give the stock price sufficient room to weather the market volatility.

As a result, the prices respond by a higher margin in the change of the overall stock valuation compared to short term trading. Besides, long term trading has a time value component.

This time value characteristic lets you rescue a little value from a depreciating contract, which would otherwise end up worthless. The overall value of an asset, security or stock under trade usually appreciates over time. The more time you have, the more time your inventory has to trend in your preferred direction and make significant returns for you.

On the other hand, short term trading has a limited number of factors to consider when making future stock speculation. Hence, your chances of getting your predictions wrong increases. In addition, short term trade quickly fluctuates in response to minor market hiccups and this lack of rigidity affects your potential profitability. Short-term contracts are risky since market trends are not easily predictable under these tight periods. Your stock has not had the necessary time to react to the different forces affecting its value.

Primary Uses for Options Investing

Trading in options is a type of investment in the stock market. However, rather than trading directly in outright stock buying and selling, you will be trading in speculative contracts. You get to make or lose your investment based on your ability to predict future market trends over a specific period. Getting involved in options trading is a decision you will have made as a strategy to grow your investment portfolio.

Unless you are an expert in the stock market, you will need the assistance and guidance of a professional broker specializing in options trading. An options broker will guide you through the ins and outs of this investment strategy. Just like any investment strategy, trading in options has an associated potential for risk. Your broker will evaluate your capital valuation and your understanding of stock markets.

Also, how much risk exposure you are worth and your ability to withstand unpredictable market shocks. Based on all these factors, he then decides on your eligibility for options trading. To minimize your risk and maximize your benefits in returns, your broker is your best source of guidelines in navigating within this investment strategy.

21. The Basics of Technical Analysis

Technical analysis is the method of using charts and other recording methods to analyze various data in options trading. Using these visual instruments, you have the chance to determine the direction of the market because they give you a trend.

This method focuses on studying the supply and demand of a market. The price will be seen to rise when the investor realizes the market is undervalued, and this leads to buying. If they think that the market is overvalued, the prices will start falling, and this is deemed the perfect time to sell.

You need to understand the movement of the various indicators to make the perfect decision. This method works on the premise that history usually repeats itself – a huge change in the prices affects the investors in any situation.

Technical analysis has been used over the years in trades. The technical analysis methods have been used for over a hundred years to come up with deductions regarding the market.

In Asia, the use of technical analysis led to the development of candlestick techniques, and it forms the main charting techniques.

Over time, more tools and techniques have come up to help traders come up with predictions of the prices in various markets.

There are many indicators that you can use to determine the direction of the market, but only a few are valuable to your course. Let us look at the various indicators and how to use them.

Support and Resistance

These levels occur at points where both the buyer and the seller aren't dormant. These levels are displayed on the chart using a horizontal line extended in the past to the future.

The different prices reach at the support and resistance points in the future.

How to Apply Support and Resistance

- Using these points allows you to know when to call or put.

- Support and resistance give you a way to determine the entry point to use for a directional trade.

The Significance of Trends in Option Trading

Technical analysis works on the premise of the trend. These trends come by due to the interaction of the buyer and the seller. The aggressiveness of one of the parties in the market will determine how steep the trend becomes. To make a profit, you have to take advantage of the changes in the price movement.

To understand the direction of the trend, you ought to look at the troughs and peaks and how they relate to each other.

When looking for money in options trading, you ought to trade with a trend. The trend is what determines the decision you make when faced with a situation – whether to buy or to sell. You need to know the various signs that a prevailing trend is soon ending so that you can manage the risks and exit the trades the right way.

Characteristics of Technical Analysis

This analysis makes use of models and trading rules using different price and volume changes. These include the volume, price, and other different market info.

Technical analysis is applied among financial professionals and traders and is used by many option traders.

The Principles of Technical analysis

Many traders on the market use the price to come up with information that affects the decision you make ultimately. The analysis looks at the trading pattern and what information it offers you rather than looking at drivers such as news events, economic and fundamental events.

Price action usually tends to change every time because the investor leans towards a certain pattern, which in turn predicts trends and conditions.

Prices Determine Trends

Technical analysts know that the price in the market determines the trend of the market. The trend can be up, down, or move sideways.

History Usually Repeats Itself

Analysts believe that an investor repeats the behavior of the people that traded before them. The investor sentiment usually repeats itself. Due to the fact that the behavior repeats itself, traders know that using a price pattern can lead to predictions.

The investor uses the research to determine if the trend will continue or if the reversal will stop eventually and will anticipate a change when the charts show a lot of investor sentiment.

Combination with Other Analysis Methods

To make the most out of the technical analysis, you need to combine it with other charting methods on the market. You also need to use secondary data, such as sentiment analysis and indicators.

To achieve this, you need to go beyond pure technical analysis, and combine other market forecast methods in line with technical work. You can use technical analysis along with fundamental analysis to improve the performance of your portfolio.

You can also combine technical analysis with economics and quantitative analysis. For instance, you can use neural networks along with technical analysis to identify the relationships in the market. Other traders make use of technical analysis with astrology.

Other traders go for newspaper polls, sentiment indicators to come with deductions.

22. Momentum Trading

Momentum is at the heart of all-day trading as finding trades with the right amount of momentum is the only way you can reliably guarantee a profit on your trades. Luckily, it is not unrealistic to expect to find at least one underlying asset that is likely to move as much as 30 percent each day due to the fact that all underlying assets with this much momentum all tend to share a few common technical indicators.

Momentum stock anatomy

While it might seem difficult to understand how anyone could expect to pick a stock with the right momentum out of the thousands of possible choices, the fact of the matter is that all high momentum stocks typically have several things in common. In fact, if you were given a list of 5,000 stocks, using the factors below you could likely come up with a list of 10 or less.

Float: The first thing you are going to want to keep in mind is that the stocks with the highest momentum are generally going to have a float that is less than 100 million shares. Float refers to the total number of shares that are currently available and can be found by taking the total number of outstanding shares and subtracting out all those that are restricted or are, functionally speaking, no longer traded. Restricted shares are those that are currently in the midst of a lockup period or other, similar restriction. The less float a stock has, the more volatility it is going to contain. Stocks with smaller float tend to have low liquidity and a higher bid/ask spread.

Daily charts: The following thing you are going to want to look for is stocks that are consistently beating their moving average and trending away from either the support or resistance depending on if you following a positive or negative trend.

Relative volume: You are also going to want to ensure that the stocks you are considering have a high amount of relative volume, with the minimum being twice what the current average is. The average you should consider in this case would be the current volume compared to the historical average for the stock in question. The standard volume is going to reset every night at midnight which means this is a great indicator when it comes to stocks that are seeing a higher than average amount of action right now.

Catalyst: While not, strictly speaking, required, you may still find it helpful to look for stocks that are currently having their momentum boosted by external sources. This can include things like activist investors, FDA announcements, PR campaigns and earnings reports.

Exit indicators to watch

Besides knowing what a potentially profitable momentum trade looks like, you are also going to need to know what to look for to ensure that you can successfully get while the getting is good. Keep the following in mind and you will always be able to get out without having to sacrifice any of your hard earned profits.

Don't get greedy: It is important to set profit targets before you go into any trade, and then follow through on them when the trade turns in your favor. If you find yourself riding a stronger trend than you initially anticipated, the best choice is to instead sell off half of your holdings before setting a new and improved price target for the rest, allowing you to have your cake and eat it too.

Red candles: If you are not quite at your price target and you come across a candle that closes in the red then this is a strong indicator that you should take what you have and exit ASAP. If you have already sold off half of your holdings at this point, however, then you are going to want to go ahead and hold through the first red candle as long as it doesn't go so far as to trigger your stop loss actively.

Extension bar: An extension bar is a candle with a spike that causes dramatically increased profits. If this occurs you want to lock in your profits as quickly as possible as it is unlikely to last very long. This is your lucky day and it is important to capitalize on it.

Choosing a screener

Another important aspect of using a momentum strategy correctly is using a quality stock screen in order to find stocks that are trending towards the extreme ends of the market based on the criteria outlined above. A good screener is a virtually indispensable tool when it comes to narrowing down the field of potential options on any given day, the best of the best even let you generate your own unique filters that display a list of stocks that meet a variety of different criteria. What follows is a list of some of the most popular screeners on the market today.

StockFetchter.com: StockFetcher.com is one of the more complicated screeners out there, but all that complexity comes with a degree of power that is difficult to beat. Its power comes from a virtually unlimited number of parameters that its users can add to filter, ensuring that you only see exactly the types of stocks you are looking for. It offers a free as well as a paid version, the free version allows you to see the top five stocks that match your parameters while the paid version, $8.95 per month, shows you unlimited results.

Finviz.com: This site offers a wide variety of different pre-made filters that are designed to return results on the most promising stocks for a given day. It is extremely user friendly as well and functions from three drop-down menus based on the type of indicator, technical, fundamental or descriptive, and lets you choose the criteria for each. The results can then be sorted in a myriad of different ways to make it as easy to find the types of stocks you are looking for as possible. The biggest downside to Finviz is that it uses delayed data which means it is going to be most effective for those who run evening screens so they are ready to go when the market opens.

Chartmill.com: This site allows users to filter stocks based on a number of predetermined criteria including things like price, performance, volume, technical indicators and candlestick patterns. It also offers up a number of more specialized indicators including things like squeeze plays, intensity, trend and pocket pivots. This site works based on a credit system, and every user is given 6,000 credits each month for free. Every scan costs a few hundred credits so you should be able to take advantage of a variety of their tools virtually free of charge. Additional credits then cost $10 per 10,000 or they have an unlimited option available for about $30 per month.

Stockrover.com: This tool is specifically designed to cater to the Canadian market in addition to the US stock market. It offers up a variety of fundamental filters in addition to technical and performance-based options. This tool also allows you to track stocks that are near their established lows and high, those that may be gaining momentum and even those that are seeing a lot of love from various hedge funds. Users also have the ability to create custom screens as well as unique equations for even more advanced screening. Users can also backtest their ideas to make sure that everything is working as intended. While their basic options are free to use, the more complex choices are gated behind a paywall that costs $250 for a year's subscription.

Know your filters

Day trading is about more than finding stocks that are high in volume, it is also about finding those that are currently experiencing a higher than average degree of movement as well. The following filters will help ensure that the stocks you find have plenty of both.

Steady volatility: In order to trade stocks that are extremely volatile with as little research as possible, the following criterion is a good place to start. It is important to use a minimum of 50 days, though 75 or 100 will produce even more reliable results overall. Results of this magnitude will show that the stock in question has moved a significant amount over the past few months which means it is likely to continue to do so for the near future. The second criterion will determine the amount you should be willing to pay per share and can be altered based on your personal preferences.

The third criterion will determine the level of volume that you find acceptable for the given timeframe. The example will look for volume that is greater than four million shares within the past month. From there, it will eliminate leverage ETFs from the results which can be eliminated if you are interested in trading ETFs. Finally, the add column will show the list of stocks with the largest amount of volume and the greatest overall amount of movement. Selecting these columns will then rank the results from least to greatest based on the criteria provided.

Monitor regularly: Alternately, you may want to do a daily search to determine the stocks that will experience the greatest range of movement in the coming hours. To do so, you will want to create a new list of stocks every evening to ensure that you will be ready to go when the market opens. This list can then be made up of stocks that have shown a higher volatility in theformer day either in terms of gains or in terms of losses. Adding in volume to these criteria will then help to make sure the results will likely continue to generate the kind of volume that day trading successfully requires. Useful filters for this search include an average volume that is greater than one million and the more you increase the minimum volume the fewer results you'll see.

When using this strategy, it is especially important to pick out any stocks that are likely to see major news releases before thefollowing day as these are almost guaranteed to make the price move in a number of random directions before ultimately settling down. As such, it is often best to wait until after the details of the release are known and you can more accurately determine what the response is, though not so long that you miss out on the combination of high volume and high volatility. If you don't already have an earnings calendar bookmarked, the one available for free from Yahoo Finance! is well respected.

Monitor intraday volatility: Another option that is worth considering is doing your researching during the day as a means of determining which stocks are experiencing the greatest overall amount of movement at the moment. A vast majority of trading platforms provide this information in real time so it is easy to keep up to date on the changes that are happening at the moment. For example, if a stock opens at a point down 10 percent from itsformer close and stays there you can then assume that there is no one biting on the action that the stock has available.

23. Cost of Doing Business

Set up an office

Asides trade losses, the greatest cost you will have as a dealer is setting up your exchanging office. Presently, this expense can fluctuate incredibly from the merchant to broker; however, at any rate, you will require a decent workstation and a PC work area and seat. A few brokers may choose a multi-screen PC arrangement and a costly PC work area and seat, which clearly could get over the top expensive. Nonetheless, this isn't important to exchange productively. All you truly need is a decent PC and a web association.

Trade losses

The primary expenses of maintaining an exchanging business are losing exchanges. Truly, it's hard to believe, but it's true, losing exchanges are and ought to be thought of as an expense of maintaining an exchanging business. It is basic you see them along these lines since it causes you to turn out to be less sincerely impacted by losing exchanges. Consider it along these lines; an eatery proprietor doesn't get tragic or irate when he needs to re-request sustenance or pay his representatives since he realizes those things are only the expenses of working together.

Along these lines, your greatest expense of business as a merchant are the misfortunes you take from losing exchanges. Each dealer on Earth, regardless of how gainful, has losing exchanges. You can't maintain a strategic distance from them, so simply acknowledge that you should manage the expense of losing exchanges and instead of attempt to keep away from them, figure out how to manage them appropriately, yet you should acknowledge them as an on-going cost first (more on the best way to manage this cost).

Another littler expense related to exchanging is that of intermediary spreads or commissions. This will be an on-going expense for you, and you ought to recollect that each time you enter an exchange, you are paying a spread or commission to your intermediary. This is a genuine expense, and you should consider it such.

You ought to likewise have a most extreme misfortune that you will acknowledge on any exchange. This is called your stop and is the place you will totally escape an exchange. There are numerous approaches to approach stops, and it mostly relies upon your style and by and large methodology (day exchanging versus swing exchanging versus position exchanging). Pick one, and after that, you can alter it as you go.

For instance, you should need to slice your misfortunes to a limit of 5% per exchange in the event that you are a swing broker. When the 5% number is broken, you are out of the exchange – regardless. You can generally get back in! On the off chance that you are a transient informal investor, possibly a $0.05 to .10 penny most extreme misfortune would be proper. Additionally, on the off chance that you are day exchanging, set a day by day misfortune limit. This is where you will quit exchanging for the afternoon. Keep in mind; the goal is to keep loss to the minimum. You can't lose cash in the event that you quit exchanging.

A few merchants additionally utilize the greatest benefit objective for the afternoon. When they achieve their objective, they quit exchanging. By and by, in the event that you quit exchanging, you can't lose cash – and you get the opportunity to keep your benefits.

There are two sorts of stops - mental and programmed. A psychological stop requires the broker to execute the exchange to close the position. A programmed stop is modified into your immediate access framework or online record. Programmed stops help remove the feeling from an exchange.

Good news and bad news

Fortunately, you realize what your expenses are, and there aren't a lot of them. Likewise, you can contain your expenses as a dealer all-around effectively and successfully. This regulation is finished by dealing with your hazard as you exchange. This implies, not gambling beyond what you can really stand to lose on any one exchange, which is finished by utilizing stop misfortunes obviously. Realizing how to place stop misfortunes appropriately will likewise be a major factor in overseeing hazards and furthermore in expanding reward. An appropriately put stop misfortune can be the contrast between a losing exchange and a triumphant exchange in numerous cases.

Presently, for the terrible news about exchanging costs. In the event that you don't oversee them and contain them appropriately, they can develop crazy, extremely, rapidly. Truth be told, on the off chance that you don't deal with your hazard appropriately as you exchange, you can wind up losing the majority of your exchanging cash incredibly, quick, quicker than in different organizations without a doubt.

Knowing this terrible news about exchanging costs, it should make you re-read the past passage again on the uplifting news of exchanging costs and advise yourself that these expenses can adequately be overseen and contained. However, it's dependent upon YOU to do it!

In this way, presently, you know the essential expenses of maintaining your exchanging business, presently, there may be others; however, these are the greatest ones for general brokers. You will likely ensure that you profit from your triumphant exchanges (income) to take care of every one of your expenses, to say the very least, so you make a benefit.

How to enhance your business profitability

As referenced already, an exchanging business keeps running at a benefit when the income (cash from winning exchanges) is counterbalancing the costs (misfortunes, office arrangement, and so forth.).

The inquiry at that point progresses toward becoming, what would you be able to do to ensure your exchanging incomes far outperform your exchanging costs? Here is an outline:

Concentrate on the hazard to compensate proportion – On each exchange you take, you have to choose if the hazard remunerates potential is sufficient to make the exchange advantageous. You should make sure at any rate a 2R or more prominent reward is conceivable while ensuring you have your stop misfortune put appropriately.

Try not to exchange a ton – You don't have to exchange with high recurrence to profit. You have to rather concentrate on figuring out how to exchange appropriately, on taking fantastic/high-likelihood exchanges. This is the point I make in my articles on exchanging like a crocodile and exchanging like a rifleman.

Concentrate more on cash management than all else – By cash management, I mean overseeing and containing your hazard per exchange and furthermore on ensuring a 2R or more noteworthy reward is conceivable and furthermore on exchange exits. Most dealers center a lot on sections and exercise in futility things like exchanging pointers when truly, they ought to be unmistakably increasingly focused on cash management.

A cash management methodology will help decide the amount to exchange. For instance, suppose you have $50,000. Would you like to enter an exchange utilizing the majority of your capital? That most likely would not be the best game-plan. On the off chance that you did, and the exchange went the incorrect way, you would assume too enormous a misfortune on one exchange. Settle on a dollar sum or level of your absolute capital that will be the most extreme you will use for any one exchange. This will help control the size of your misfortunes. Numerous fruitful merchants use 3%-5% as the greatest per exchange.

Ensure you know how to read a price chart appropriately – If it happens that you don't understand how to read a price diagram, you aren't going to get much of anywhere. The premise of any effective trading business is knowing the price elements and how to read and also trade from pure price movement.

24. Step by step Instructions to Profit from Buying

Options merchants can benefit by being an alternative purchaser or an option essayist. Alternatives take into consideration potential benefit during both unpredictable occasions, and when the market is peaceful or less unstable. This is conceivable in light of the fact that the costs of benefits like stocks, monetary standards, and items are continually moving, and regardless of what the economic situations are. there is an option methodology that can exploit it.

Rudiments of Options Profitability

A call alternative purchaser stands to make a benefit if the fundamental resource, suppose a stock, transcends the strike cost before expiry. A put options purchaser makes a benefit if the value falls underneath the strike cost before the termination. The precise measure of benefit relies upon the distinction between the stock cost and the alternative strike cost at lapse or when the options position is shut.

A call alternative author stands to make a benefit if the basic stock remains beneath the strike cost. In the wake of composing a put alternative, the dealer benefits if the value remains over the strike cost. An option essayist's gainfulness is restricted to the exception they get for composing the options (which is the options purchaser's expense). Options essayists are additionally called options dealers.

An alternative purchaser can make a significant quantifiable profit if the options exchange works out. This is on the grounds that a stock cost can move fundamentally past the strike cost.

This investigation avoids alternative places that were finished off or practiced before termination. All things being equal, for each alternative agreement that was in the cash (ITM) at lapse, there were three that were out of the cash (OTM), and in this way, useless is a really telling measurement.

Here's a straightforward test to assess your hazard resilience so as to decide if you are in an ideal situation being an alternative purchaser or an option author. Suppose you can purchase or compose 10 call alternative agreements, with the cost of each call at $0.50. Each agreement regularly has 100 offers as the basic resource, so 10 agreements would cost $500 ($0.50 x 100 x 10 agreements).

On the off chance that you purchase 10 call options agreements, you pay $500, and that is the greatest misfortune that you can cause. Nonetheless, your potential benefit is hypothetically boundless. So, what's the trick? The probability of the exchange being gainful isn't exceptionally high. While this likelihood relies upon the suggested unpredictability of the call alternative and the time frame staying to termination, suppose it's 25%.

Then again, in the event that you compose 10 call options agreements, your most extreme benefit is the measure of the top-notch salary, or $500, while your misfortune is hypothetically boundless. Be that as it may, the chances of the alternatives exchange being productive are particularly in support of you, at 75%.

So, would you hazard $500, realizing that you have a 75% shot of losing your speculation and a 25% possibility of making a benefit? Or on the other hand, would you like to make a limit of $500, realizing that you have a 75% shot of keeping the whole sum or part of it, however, have a 25% possibility of the exchange being a losing one?

The response to those inquiries will give you a thought of your hazard resilience and whether you are in an ideal situation being an option purchaser or options essayist.

It is essential to remember that these are the general insights that apply to all options, however, at specific occasions, it might be increasingly useful to be an alternative essayist or a purchaser in a particular resource. Applying the correct procedure at the ideal time could change these chances essentially.

While calls and puts can be joined in different changes to frame modern options procedures, how about we assess the hazard/reward of the four most essential methodologies.

Purchasing a Call

This is the most essential options system. It is a generally okay system, since the most extreme misfortune is confined to the premium paid to purchase the call, while the greatest reward is conceivably boundless. In spite of the fact that, as expressed prior, the chances of the exchange being entirely beneficial are ordinarily genuinely low. "Generally safe" expect that the complete expense of the alternative speaks to a little level of the dealer's capital. Taking a chance with all capital on a solitary call alternative would make it an exceptionally unsafe exchange, since all the cash could be lost if the options terminates useless.

Purchasing call options is a bullish technique utilizing influence and is a hazard characterized option in contrast to buying stock. Prior the conceptual "call options give the purchaser the privilege; however not the commitment to summon stock", a commonsense delineation will be given:

A merchant is bullish on a specific stock trade at $50.

The broker is either chance or gaining, needing to know beforehand their most extreme misfortune or needs greatly influence than basically owning stock.

Purchasing a Put

This is another procedure which is generally okay; however, the conceivably high reward if the exchange works out. Purchasing puts is a practical option in contrast to the less secure system of short selling the hidden resource. Puts can likewise be purchased to fence drawback chance in a portfolio. But since value records normally pattern higher after some time, which implies that stocks by and large will in general advance more regularly than they decay, the hazard/compensate profile of the put purchaser is marginally less ideal than that of a call purchaser.

What to Consider When Buying Put Options in Stock Trading

When you purchase a put alternative, you're trusting that the cost of the basic stock falls. You profit with puts when the cost of the alternative ascents, or when you practice the options to purchase the stock at a value that is beneath the strike cost and afterward sell the stock in the open market, stashing the distinction. By purchasing a put option, you limit your danger of a misfortune to the superior that you paid for the put.

In the event that, for instance, you purchased an ABC December 50 put, and ABC tumbles to $40 per share, you can profit either by selling a put options that ascents in cost or by purchasing the stock at $40 on the open market and afterward practicing the options, accordingly selling your $40 stock to the author for $50 per share, which is what owning the put gave you the privilege to do.

Composing a Put

Put composing is a favored system of cutting-edge options brokers, since in the most dire outcome imaginable, the stock is appointed to the put author (they need to purchase the stock), while the most ideal situation is that the essayist holds everything of the alternative premium. The greatest danger of put composing is that the essayist may wind up paying a lot for a stock on the off chance that it tanks in this way. The hazard/compensate profile of put composing is more horrible than that of put or call purchasing, since the most extreme reward rises to the premium got, yet the greatest misfortune is a lot higher. So, as examined formerly, the likelihood of having the option to make a benefit is higher.

Composing a Call

Call composing comes in two structures, secured and bare. Secured call composing is another most loved system of middle of the road to cutting edge options merchants, and is commonly used to create additional salary from a portfolio. It includes composing approaches stocks held inside the portfolio. Revealed or exposed call composing is the restrictive territory of hazard tolerant, modern alternatives brokers, as it has a hazard profile like that of a short deal in stock. The most extreme reward in call composing is equivalent to the premium gotten. The greatest hazard with a secured call system is that the hidden stock will be "summoned." With stripped call composing, the most extreme misfortune is hypothetically boundless, similarly for what it's worth with a short deal.

Alternatives Spreads

Customarily, dealers or financial specialists will join alternatives utilizing a spread system, getting at least one options to sell at least one unique option. Spreading will counterbalance the premium paid in light of the fact that the sold alternative premium will net against the options premium obtained. Besides, the hazard and return profiles of a spread will top out the potential benefit or misfortune. Spreads can be made to exploit about any foreseen value activity, and can extend from the easy to the complex. Likewise, with individual options, any spread procedure can be either purchased or sold.

Financial specialists and brokers embrace alternative exchanging either to support open situations (for instance, purchasing puts to fence a long position, or purchasing calls to support a short position) or to hypothesize on likely value developments of a fundamental resource.

The greatest advantage of utilizing alternatives is that of influence. For instance, say a speculator has $900 to use on a specific exchange and wants the most value for-the-money. The speculator is bullish in the present moment on XYZ Inc. Thus, expect XYZ is exchanging at $90. Our financial specialist can purchase a limit of 10 portions of XYZ. Notwithstanding, XYZ additionally has three-month calls accessible with a strike cost of $95 for an expense of $3. Presently, rather than purchasing the offers, the speculator purchases three call options agreements. Purchasing three call options will cost $900 (3 agreements x 100 offers x $3).

In a matter of seconds before the call options lapse, assume XYZ is exchanging at $103 and the calls are exchanging at $8, so all in all, the financial specialist sells the calls. Here's the means by which the arrival on venture piles up for each situation.

Inside and out acquisition of XYZ shares at $90: Profit = $13 per share x 10 offers = $130 = 14.4% return ($130/$900).

Acquisition of three $95 call options agreements: Profit = $8 x 100 x 3 agreements = $2,400 less premium paid of $900 = $1500 = 166.7% return ($1,500/$900).

Obviously, the hazard with purchasing the calls as opposed to the offers is that if XYZ had not exchanged above $95 by alternative termination, the calls would have lapsed useless and all $900 would be lost. Truth be told, XYZ needed to exchange at $98 ($95 strike cost + $3 premium paid), or about 9% higher from its cost when the calls were acquired, for the exchange just to break even. At the point when the merchant's expense to put the exchange is likewise added to the condition to be productive, the stock would need to exchange significantly higher.

These situations expect that the dealer held till termination. That isn't required with American alternatives. Whenever before expiry, the broker could have offered the alternative to secure a benefit. Or on the other hand, in the event that it looked the stock was not going to move over the strike value, they could sell the alternative for its outstanding time an incentive, so as to lessen the misfortune.

25. Swing Trading Strategies

There are specific strategies that you can put in place so that you will identify a trading opportunity. You will be in a position to manage your deals from the word go. You will know the stock you can invest in so that you see the potential in price that will be there in the market. You will know both the present and in the future. There are strategies that you can put in place so that you will have a productive trade.

Fibonacci Retracement

The strategy will help you to know the level of support as well as resistance. You will be in a position to establish whether there will be a possibility of a price reverse pattern.

Support as well as Resistance Triggers

When you know the things that trigger resistance as well as the support in the trading swing, you will be in a position to trade best. You will know how to turn them into strengths, and they will work in your favor. The buying levels higher to the extent of overcoming the selling pressure. At times, the buying pressure is much that it will surpass the selling. When this occurs, the price decline is halted, making the prices to turn back upwards. You need to know the exact time that you have to bring in the support as well as a resistance strategy.

Channel Trading

You need to identify a stock that will display the first movement and dealing within the channel. Make sure that you conduct trade within the trend. When the price takes a downward trend, you need to find for a sell position. Looking for a sell position is significant no unless the price will break out of the pattern. That will mean that it will go to a higher level and showing a reversal when an upward movement begins.

10- and 20-Day SMA

Here is where you make use of the simple moving strategies. The strategy will help you to calculate a constant updating price which will go past a specific period. That will help you to make sure that the price data is smooth as things go on. That will mean that you will add up the closing price of ten days and then divide with ten. You will get the average price out of the ten days. All the averages are connected, and that will create a smooth trend that will make sure that all things go as you have planned. Simple moving averages that have short lengths will have a likelihood of reacting faster to the change in prices than the ones with a more extended period. When the ten closes the twenty, there is a buying signal that will generate as an indication that the prices will go up in a short time. When the ten goes crosses below the twenty, a selling signal will be seen to show that there will be a downward trend in some time to come.

The MACD Crossover

It is a great way to help you to identify the opportunities that are there in the swing trade. It is the most popular strategy that will help you to indicate the direction a particular trend is taking. Whether it is a reversal of an upward movement and has two averages that move from time to time. When the two standards cross, they will lead to the generation of the buying as well as selling signals. The two lines are as well likely to cross above the signal line you have the opportunity to get into the trade. That will enable you to buy any item that you need. Wait for the two paths to cross, and they will create a signal for a business in the opposite direction. You need to be quick before the swing traders withdraw from the trade. These strategies can be put into use and will help you to know the trading opportunities that are there in any market that you have an interest in. Use the best approach to apply these strategies, and you will benefit significantly from them. Seek to find out more about swing trade and the technical indicators and the signals that they show. You will be in a position to predict the price pattern both in the present time as well as in the future.

Trailing Stop and Stop-Loss Combo

There are brokers out there in the market who will do all they can afford so that investors will not suffer much loss. Stop-loss-order is a strategy that is widely known and will always protect you from suffering huge losses. It the price goes down to a certain level, the share will be sold regardless of the current price in the market to make sure that there will be no other losses. For stop-loss to be effective, it needs to be paired with a trailing stop. A trailing stop is a trade order, and it means that the stop-loss price is not fixed to a single dollar amount but is set at a particular percentage or amount that is below the current market price. When the prices shoot, the trailing stop as well goes up. In situations where the price is not rising any longer, the stop-loss will remain in the same place. That will be a way to shield an investor from suffering losses, and there will be profits realized since the price will get to higher levels.

You can apply trailing-stop in stock, options as well as future exchanges that are there to support the traditional stop-loss orders. You can calculate the maximum risk tolerance when you bring together the conventional stop-losses as well as trailing stops. When the price of a share does up, the trailing-stop will go above the fixed stop-loss, making it be obsolete.

When there is a further price increment, it will mean minimizing the potential losses more. There is an added protection, and that will mean that the trailing-stop will take an upward movement. During the regular market hours, trailing will calculate the stop's triggers with consistency.

The trailing stop is hard to apply with active trade because of price fluctuations and the level of the volatility of the particular stock. Fast-moving stock attracts traders because it has the potential to bring forth substantial profit in a short period. For active trade to be useful, a trailing stop value that ca accommodate the usual price fluctuation should be set. Before you get in business, you need to know how the market is for this strategy to work. Being able to time your trade correctly, and it will be of much importance. The trailing-stop is an excellent tool for eliminating and separating you from the emotional part of it that can be in trading. You will be in a position to make the right decisions that you will base on statistical information. There can be lost when you decide to use trailing loss on its own. When you combine with stop-loss, it will be an excellent idea to minimize losses as well as protecting profits.

The idea will help you to reduce losses, get more profit, and the trade will move in your favor. You can choose to use trailing stop in day trading or not to use. The stop-loss order is an approach to use when you want to control the risk levels in a market. If the market is not stable and the prices move in the opposite direction, you can opt to withdraw from the trade. When trailing-stop-loss, you will run the stop-loss up, and the stock price will move upwards. When the price of stock is heading in the right direction, the risk of trade will reduce. When you decide to take a short position in business, and you have a stop-loss, and you decide to trail it, it will be possible. However, you need to wait for the prices to go down.

You need to be careful not to move the stop-loss-order if at all, you are in a short position. That will make you experience massive losses, and you may go to the extent of leaving the trade.

Broker Risk

In some cases, you need something, and you are not sure where to get it. You may be torn in between two things, and you are not sure which is the best. In such a case, you need a broker to help you out. A broker is a middleman who will be in charge of bringing together a buyer and the seller. You will mostly find the brokers in the business world, and they broke aiming to get some commission. A broker can either be a person or a company, and they will arrange transactions on your behalf. They can either be insurance, a commodity as well as stockbrokers.

A broker will be responsible for bringing forth a seller or a buyer and will transact on their behalf. But there are no cases where we can represent them at the same time. They will either provide you with information as well as advice pertaining a particular trade. They will do that at a cost, and that is where they mostly get their income from. That means they have a lot of information and will invest a lot so that they can know more about the trade they are in.

A broker will aim at establishing a relationship with a lot of people that seem to be prospective clients. They will do all in their reach so that they can have the best connections with both the sellers and the buyers in trade and conducts the best deals ever. Research is part of what they do from time to time so that they can have full information at their disposal. Brokers will analyze raw data to establish whether a particular investment is an excellent risk. They will do all they can to provide resources that will help you to manage risk.

They will have full knowledge of what is risk management and how to go about it. They will have numerous solutions for you when it comes to managing risk and ensuring that you minimize the risk associated with a particular trade. They will do all they can to provide you the services that you need. Fixing the risk management tools is what they are best in until it is compatible with the sales process. A broker will not hesitate to teach you or their client how to profit when they apply the risk management tools in the right way. They will do all they can to promote the risk management approaches within the company that they represent in the market. Risk management comes with certain benefits that the brokers are well aware of. You will understand how the whole process will take place with their help. They will know the possible triggers that will interrupt trade, and they will know how to handle each to minimize the possibility of losses.

A broker is a lifesaver. Nevertheless, they can do the things that they are not instructed by the risk management team to do. They will do some things to make sure you are entirely out of the market, and they are there to represent you if you need to go back. Some risks will come along with the broker, and you need to be extra careful when you are dealing with one.

26. Some Case Studies

Case studies allow traders to have a clearer understanding of the options strategies and the outcomes to expect so that they can avoid the errors or take up the same steps that the traders in the case study used. Here are a few case studies to provide you with a practical approach to options trading:

Case Study #1

This is a study of a metal works company that is concerned about the rising prices of one of its critical inputs, steel. The current market price of the steel is $400 per ton, but the manufacturer is afraid that the price could rise and get to more than $500 per ton.

To remedy the situation, the investor decided to buy a call option at $500 per ton. The call option strike price is equivalent to the forecast threshold that the investor is worried about.

Once he purchases the call option, the investor pays a premium to the writer of the option so that if the market price does not go above the $500 per ton, the option will expire out-of-the-money. If this happens, the investor will not experience too much loss when the option expires because he will still be able to buy his steel below the $500 threshold. The only loss he will incur is the premium he paid to the writer of the option.

In the event the market price exceeds $500 per ton, the option will expire in-the-money, and the option holder will make a profit from it. For example, if the price goes as high as $550 per pound of steel, the investor will exercise his option and will purchase a ton of steel at $500, from the option writer. He makes a profit of his savings, less the premium he paid. In case the premium was $10, the profit will be $40. This is found by ($550 -$500) - $10. Hence, the investor will be protected against the steel price going above $500 per ton.

In this example, the call option serves as a hedge against the changes in the steel market. The call option's interactions remain the same despite the changes in the market. In the investor's case above, it is clear that the out-of-money option puts a limit to the downside to the premium paid on the option, $10. All market prices will experience a downside up to, and including, premium and the strike price. However, once the market price exceeds the sum of the premium and the strike price, the investor will enjoy a profit. Luckily, the profit or the upside is unlimited.

In this example, the option purchased will have been a successful hedge against an anticipated rise in the price of steel. The call option limits the downside to the price of the premium but maintains an open door to the profits through the unlimited upside.

Case Study #2

Here's a case study borrowed from the Terry Tips blog.

Costco had begun trading in 2015 at $141.87, and at that time, Terry Tips' portfolio, one that uses COST as the underlying asset, was valued at $6223. Had this money been devoted, it would have produced 43.8 shares or roughly 44 shares of the stock.

Early in that year, the price rose steadily but fell from a $153 high to a $135 low within the first week of September. By the end of that month, the stock was now trading at $3 higher than it had traded when the year began.

If you were to compare the value of the 44 COST shares and the current value of the Terry Tips portfolio had it traded options in that same period, the situation could have been as follows:

When the stock fell a little in January, the value of the portfolio could the value of the portfolio followed and fell by an even more considerable amount. However, as the value of the stock recovered, the portfolio outdid it again and outperformed on the upside also.

Over the nine months between January and September, investing in stocks could only have produced returns of $1.20 per share, which means that for the 44 shares, the investor would have received $52.80. The stock obtained $2.70 per share above the 9-months that the 44 shares would have increased their worth by $118.80 compared to their value at the beginning of the year. This increase translates to a $171.60 net gain, adding the $52.80 dividends paid out. The net gain represents a 1.2% gain in the value of the stocks in 9 months.

Above the equal period, the definite COST options portfolio had risen in value to $12,900 from $6,223, a net gain of $6,667, which represents a 107% increased value.

Looking at the trading strategy used, Terry Tips owned seven calls, all of which expired in April, and two others that would extend until July. They had also sold 8 calls that expired on January 15, of which 3 had a strike price just under the stock value, while the remaining 5 were somewhat out-of-the-money. The company also have 1 long uncovered call against, that they could have sold a short-term call; nevertheless, they thought it better to maintain a higher net delta. With that portfolio, and with different options positions, Terry Tips owned about 218 shares of stock, which does not compare to directly owning 44 shares.

By the end of the nine months, on September 25, all the long calls had been pushed to January to April of the following year, 2016, and the company still held a few put positions. In May, when the COST shares were selling at $144, the company had sold a bullish credit put spread. (It had bought October-15 135 puts but sold October-15 140 puts). Terry Tips figured that if the price were above $140 at the time when the puts expire on October 16, the puts would have been rendered worthless, and the company would have 51% on the quantity it had risked when it sold its spread in May.

Halfway through 2015, Terry Tips decided to switch tactics and change how it traded its portfolio. By now, they were now short some weekly options for numerous dissimilar series. Therefore, individual week, when some calls would expire, Terry Tips would repurchase them on a Friday, typically, and then sell the new ones, which would have a four-week time limit.

The company was careful to pick out only the strikes that would balance out its risk profile by carefully weighing its portfolio. This also gave them the opportunity to tweak its investment profile each week, and to make small changes, rather than waiting to make some grand alterations at the end of the month when the options expired. The company credits its superior performance while managing the profile to its style of trading, saying that it would not have been possible had the company not taken up the weekly options.

At the end of every week, on Friday, the company would create a risk-profile graph so that it would act as the guide in helping them choose the strike prices to use when it buys back the expiring weekly options to change them with new short calls whose expiry was further out.

The value gained from trading options does not compare to one gained trading stocks. With a starting value of $6,223, the company realized a 107% portfolio gain, even higher than the income the investors started with. A person who chose to invest in stocks by buying COST shares safely would only have gained $172, 1.2% of his portfolio. The options portfolio outperformed the gains from the stocks so many times over.

The Terry Tips example clearly illustrates, beyond all doubt, that when options strategies are correctly executed, they can out-perform the direct shares purchase. Indeed, it is much easier to buy stock, and it involves less risk, but although trading options is demanding and involves much more risks, it is sure worth investing it because, with attention and time, it performs many times better than shares.

Case Study #3

Let's see how this second case compares to the COST investment example (both made by Terry Tips).

Terry Tips decided to invest in Starbucks because its stock had been doing so well, particularly in the first 9 months of the year 2015. At the beginning of the year, the stock started at $81.44 then rose steadily to $98 before the two for one stock split in early April. By the end of the ninth month, September, the stock was trading at $57.99, which got to $115.98 as the pre-split price. Starbucks paid three $.16 dividend then paid another $0.48 to the total adding up to a total of $35.02, which translates to a 43% gain in the 9 months.

Terry Tips started the year by investing $6032 and invested in Starbucks options. Had they purchased the shares themselves, at $81.44 per share, the company would only have afforded to purchase 74 shares. In only 9 months, the portfolio would have procured $11,768 or 195% in value.

Unfortunately, Terry Tips' portfolio did not gain much because they had also invested an equal amount with the Keurig Green Mountain (GMCR), another coffer company. Over the same period, the GMCR portfolio lost $8905 because the stock value fell from $130 to $50s. However, the company did drop GMCR stock in August, and the company added FB to its portfolio, now dealing with FB and Starbucks stock, but in separate portfolios.

The portfolio established at the beginning of the year reached $10,604, and by the end of the nine months, it had gone up to $12,708. The value increase was $2182, which is 20.5%. This was a small, though not bad, value gain over the 9 months, considering that the market had fallen by 6.7%. However, this does not compare to the 195% the company would have enjoyed had it stuck to the Starbucks investment alone.

The three case studies described above are enough proof that if options strategies are correctly executed, they can outright outperform the direct bought of shares, by numerous times over. Absolutely, it's safe, uncomplicated, and less demanding to choose to invest in the stock, but if you are willing to put in the work, by giving your portfolio the time, the attention, and the research it demands. You will end up earning profits of 195% instead of a mere 43%, or 107%, rather than 1.2% with the same investment, using the same stock.

If you wish to take up options trading but don't have the time or the knowledge you would require to run a self-directed options trading account, opt for the auto-trade services that most brokers offer. The trades will be made automatically for you, and although you might have to pay some commission, it doesn't compare to getting the 1.2% returns you would get investing in stocks under the buy-and-hold setup.

27. Earning Income with Credit Spreads

Time decay and the expiration date are things that work to our advantage rather than being things to worry about. If the strategy is implemented carefully, it is possible to generate a reliable income from week-to-week or monthly. You can use different ways to earn your money depending on how you want to do it.

There is a risk of assignment but it will actually below if you setup your spreads carefully. In addition, we are using spreads to mitigate the risk. As we will see below doing it this way means that we will be able to limit the risk of assignment and if that happens it will all be automatic and our risks and total losses will be limited.

Contrary to public opinion, this is a low-risk strategy if it is done correctly.

Put Credit Spread Basic Setup

The idea of a put credit spread starts with a similar idea that we saw in the case of a debit spread. That is, we are going to be buying and selling two options simultaneously. They are both going to be the same type (in this case put options) and they are going to have the same expiration date. However, they are going to have different strike prices.

The difference between a credit and a debit spread is that this time we are looking to sell an option that has a higher strike price, and hence more valuable. In the case of a debit spread, the goal is to earn money from the stock price declining. In the case of a put credit spread, we are only hoping that the stock price remains above the higher strike price in our spread. We are not going to earn money from the price movement of the stock, this is an income-generating situation. So we don't really care what the stock does other than hoping that it is going to remain above the higher strike price of the two options. So although some people talk about this as being a "bull" credit spread, or a "bet" that the stock price is going to rise, it really isn't either of those things. If the stock price drops some, but it stays above our strike price, we are still going to make money. In fact, all we really care about is that it stays above the break even price.

The risk that is associated with a put credit spread is that the stock will drop by a large amount, that turns out to be big enough so that it drops below the upper strike price in the spread. We will look at the risks involved in detail below.

When NOT to sell a put credit spread

There are certain situations that you want to avoid selling a put credit spread. Under normal conditions, selling put credit spreads is a low-risk activity. However, if you are in a situation where the stock is moving by a large amount, with a lot of selloffs, then it is higher risk.

For that reason, you don't want to sell put credit spreads that are going to be active after an earnings call. As we noted on straddles and strangles, an earnings call is one of those times when stock can move by huge amounts. If the stock moves up by a large amount, your put credit spread would be unaffected. If the stock stays about the same or only moves by a small amount, your put credit spread would also be unaffected. But, if the earnings call was negative earnings call that really disappointed investor, the stock price may fall by large amounts – and put your higher strike price put in the money. With that in mind, you want to be conscious of when the earnings call dates are for the companies that you are investing in. And avoid selling put credit spreads during those weeks. Earnings calls are staggered, so when you are on the sidelines with one stock you can be investing in a different stock by selling put credit spreads.

There are other events that can cause your put credit spread to be at risk. A major downturn in the overall market can certainly do so. When the market starts dropping, most stocks are going with it (otherwise the market would not be dropping), and nobody really knows when the stock is going to bottom out. So if this is an ongoing process it might be better to wait on the sidelines or even switch to selling some call credit spreads, which we will discuss below.

However, even in bad markets selling put credit spreads can work. Many very successful traders earned good money continuing to sell put credit spread s(or naked puts as well) during the 2008 financial crisis. The problem with this is you have to be very smart about what you use for your strike prices. Most people will find it easier to switch to selling call credit spreads during these types of situations, including mere "corrections."

Often bad news is hard to predict. At the time of writing, there has been a parade of bad news (as far as the markets are concerned) in the form of what can be described as extrinsic events. That is, these are events that are outside the stock market itself. For example, Trump is involved in his trade war with China. That may or may not be a positive thing, but the markets aren't very happy about it and would like to see a deal worked out. So every time that Trump tweets about raising tariffs, the market goes through a major drop. That could put your positions at risk if you are selling put options. But again, choosing carefully can help avoid too much risk. Also, you can always get out of a position, something that we will be discussing.

The purpose of this trade is to earn income

When you enter into a put credit spread, you get paid for it. The purpose of doing this trade is to earn income. You actually won't see the money until the position is closed. The position can be closed at expiration, or you can close it early by buying it back. So remember that you enter into a position of a put credit spread by selling it.

Let's look at some real examples. You can sell a put credit spread for Facebook using the strike prices $170/$155 expiring on 3/20/20, and you would get paid $435. The break even price is $165.67. The current share price is $183.45, and so unless something major happens between the time you enter the position and the time you close it out, it is unlikely that you are going to have to worry about the break-even price. Of course, a lot of politicians are babbling about breaking up the tech companies lately, so that could cut into your potential profits in the case of Facebook.

The maximum loss for this put credit spread is $1,065. Your broker will require you to put up $1,065 as coal for this position. They are not going to withdraw the money from your account. Again, this is because you are selling the spread. But your buying power will be reduced by that amount until you close the position.

That one expires a long time from now, but you can setup put credit spreads that expire in a few days. For example, a put credit spread with strike prices of $182 and $180 that expires in 9 days will pay you $82. The maximum loss is $168. In this case, you would have to put up $168 in coal.

Now, $82 might not sound like much. But consider the fact that you can enter into as many contracts as you like, and with a highly prized stock like Facebook it's going to be easy to sell them. So you could do ten contracts, and that would give you an income for the week of $820. Not bad for a passive income (well, mostly passive, you should be keeping up with your trades).

An Income Strategy

Of course, you also have to put up coal for all ten contracts, so that would mean you'd need $1,680 in your account to cover the trades. But this is really an amazing return when you think about it. There is simply no other way to earn money like this. You only have to tie up the $1,680 for about 9 days, and then you'll earn $820 – so you could think of this as a 49% return in just 9 days. Of course, we note for the record that these transactions are not without risk.

As an income strategy, what you would want to do is enter into these types of positions every single week. So that would mean using the coal you have in your account to generate income week after week repeatedly. Of course, this is not automatic or magic, you are going to have to be careful about the positions you enter and be ready to close them early if they look like they are going bad, to mitigate losses. But many people actually use this strategy to make a living as options traders. Some people use 45 days or one-month time frames, others use about a week as described, and others even sell options on the expiration day. Remember that when you are working with a stock or exchange traded fund that is in high demand, there is always going to be a buyer out there somewhere. We don't have to worry about their motivations for taking the contracts off our hands, our only concern is going to be being able to get out of the trades when we need to. If the stock prices are very favorable then you can just let them expire.

You can increase your weekly or monthly income by putting up more coal. Consider the difference between doing it this way and selling a protected put. If Facebook is trading at $183 a share, for a protected put, we would have to tie up around $18,300 for a put option that expired in 9 days with a $182 strike price, as coal. If we sold a $180 strike price put, We would only earn $239 for the trouble.

When you compare that to the put credit spread, where we can sell ten contracts and earn $820, but only tie up $1,680 in coal, you have to ask why would anyone bother selling a protected put? In my view, there isn't any reason to sell protected puts. In fact, if you have $18k that you can sink in the stock market to use as coal, you should probably be selling naked put options.

28. Passive Income

There are, broadly speaking, two ways of making money. The first is to exchange your time for money and the second is to exchange your money for money. The first way is to undertake something like a job or to freelance. You're investing your time into a project and in return you get paid. Yes, you're really getting paid for a result if you're freelancing but my point is that it takes time to produce that result.

The more time you spend on such tasks, the more your earning ability is. If you're a freelance writer, for example, the greater the number of high-quality words you produce, the more you're going to get paid per month. Thus, one of the important things to note about this sort of income is that when you go to sleep, so does your income stream.

When asked about one of the key things that rich people do that poor people don't, Bill Gates responded by saying that the rich leverage their time a lot better (Bodnar, 2017). What does leverage time mean? Well, Gates' point was that the only thing that is truly limited in our lives is time. We cannot get back the time we've lost, no matter how much we would like to believe that time machines exist.

So ultimately, being financially successful comes down to how well you manage your time. The fact of the matter is that a rich person manages to get paid more for a unit of their time than a poor person does. So how do you get paid more per hour?

Leveraging Time

One easy way is to up skill yourself. Simply learn a higher skill and work in a more lucrative field. However, even this doesn't fully leverage your time since once you go to sleep, your money tap is switched off. Hence, the thing to do is to create multiple streams of income. If you have two streams of income paying you at the same time, you can double your hourly wage.

The problem is that you can only do so much at once. You can't perform two jobs at the same moment of time. So what you really want is another source of income that doesn't place demands on your time which will detract you from your job or hourly source of money. This is precisely what a passive income stream is.

Passive streams leverage your time by simply providing you with an additional amount of money for no additional input of time. I want to make something clear at this point; you will need to spend time creating and maintaining the passive income stream. My point is that your earning ability with this stream doesn't directly depend on how many hours you put into it.

If you spend five hours writing, you're going to get paid for the words you produced in those five hours. If you spend five hours on a passive income stream, you're not going to get paid for those five hours necessarily. You could get paid less, you could get paid more, who knows? The point is that whatever comes, adds to your income as long as you spend the time to do things correctly.

For example, a savings account provides you with passive income. A real estate investment on which you earn rent provides you with passive income. You can spend ten hours a day maintaining your property or spend two hours, it doesn't matter. It will earn you the market level of rent as long as things are maintained properly. There is an aspect of marginal utility with passive income, as economists call it (Bloomenthal, 2019).

Marginal utility refers to the return you receive, in satisfaction or dollars, for every unit of work spent. So, if you spend five hours fixing the taps, that is probably going to make you good money. Spending an additional hour figuring out which exact shade of white the walls need to be painted with is probably not going to make you much. Hence, the marginal utility of the former is a lot higher than the latter.

All passive income streams have a level of maximum marginal utility before the returns start dropping off. Trading options, if you're catching on, is subject to the same forces. Remember that your return is measured not just in money but also in the satisfaction and quality of life you receive. So, you need to figure out this value first.

A good way of understanding the value you'll receive and checking which style of trading you wish to adopt is to understand the styles of trading themselves. This way, you can make an accurate judgment of what suits you best.

Active and Passive Trading

As far as the SEC is concerned, all trading is active. Passive actions are reserved for the investment world. Whatever the good folk of the SEC might think, in reality, there are active forms of trading as well as passive forms. The diversity of the markets means that there exist many ways in which you can divide trading activity. Active versus passive simply happens to be one method of doing so.

Active trading refers to what you think traders actually do. This is where people sit glued to their terminals waiting on tenterhooks for news items to be released and then acting like hotshots when they make money. All of this is accurate except for that last bit which is a caricature. Either way, active trading usually involves taking directional bets on the market and usually hedging that with some other financial instrument.

Institutional traders, the kinds that trade for hedge funds, big banks and proprietary trading firms (prop shops), are all active traders. No matter what sort of strategies they employ and no matter which instruments they trade, they're always in touch with the markets. They need to be this way because their objective is to squeeze every ounce of money available.

In order to do so, they have to follow the market's every move. They need to know the market backwards and cannot have things sneak up on them. What's more, they need to deal with unexpected things that happen over holidays or weekends. For example, as of this writing, oil traders around the world have had to deal with the repercussions of a couple of

Saudi Arabian oil fields being attacked.

This happened over the weekend and when the markets were closed. As they returned to work on Monday, you can bet that none of them had slept through the weekend. Active traders tend to look at this sort of thing as an opportunity. Market mispricing happen during such events and opportunities present themselves. One needs to love the adrenaline rush that occurs during such times. It's no surprise then, that at big banks, the average trader spends about five years on a desk before moving onto a managerial position where they supervise other traders who ultimately place all the bets.

It just isn't easy keeping up with such a lifestyle, after all. In contrast to this active trader, we have the passive trader. The passive trader's returns are not comparable to the active one's. This doesn't mean they make less money, just that they make less than the average active trader.

The trade off is that they get to spend their time doing something else. Understandably, a lot of big banks look down upon this sort of thing since a good quality of life on the trading desk usually means losses. However, some hedge funds and other private institutions welcome this sort of thing actively.

You see, a holy grail in the financial world is the pursuit of market neutral returns. Market neutral means that the strategy makes money no matter what the market does. In such strategies, a trader sets things up via complex financial instruments and then lets the market play itself out. This doesn't mean they go to sleep after this, they simply recycle the strategy in as many markets as possible.

Thus, while the strategy is passive the trader is active by choice in such institutions. There are sole traders who fix their level of activity within prop shops by trading this way. There is a lot of freedom in such strategies since the trader is not chained to their desk out of necessity. They can vary their involvement in the market and while the returns don't compare to active strategies, the overall payoff is worth it to the trader.

Almost every passive strategy involves the use of options. The ones that don't involve the usage of derivatives that behave like options.

Pros and Cons of Passive Income

While there seem to be a lot of positives from passive income, I must warn you that it isn't all a bed of roses. Even roses have thorns, after all. The negatives that lend themselves to passive income almost entirely have to do with how people approach it. A lot of people think that this is lazy money and that things run on autopilot.

Well, this is not the case at all. Every passive income stream, including the ones to do with trading require investment of either time or money or both. In the case of passive trading income, you need to invest both. Time is needed to learn and study the markets and to develop your skills.

The markets are not easily deciphered mainly because they are chaotic. Our brains are designed to handle linear environments and understand step by step patterns easily. However, patterns that present themselves intermittently, rhyming with one another instead of replicating themselves exactly, are an alien language.

Thankfully, our brains are learning machines and over time, we can learn to spot such patterns. This is really what trading is all about. Time is needed to train your brain to get used to this new world where everything happens at random but plays out according to a perfectly predictable bigger picture.

Therefore, you need to spend time learning the markets and understanding the ins and outs of options. You need to learn their characteristics to such an extent that you should instantly be able to decide whether to adjust a trade or not. Options trades are complex on the surface since they involve at least two legs. Adjustment is a case of removing both legs or just one and establishing another leg elsewhere.

This calls for mental agility, so you need to spend time to work up to this level. Do not expect to be able to do this overnight. The other thing to invest into this is money. This is simple enough to understand. You need money to trade and as mentioned earlier, your level of capitalization is going to determine how long you can survive.

This sounds like a bleak thing to say but it's better to assume the worst in these situations in order to set yourself up for long term success. This way, there's no chance you'll ever take this endeavor lightly. Now that I've addressed the negatives, let's look at the positives.

Simply put, passive income can make you money while you sleep. It also frees up your time to do more things since you'll eventually reach a stage where your passive income exceeds your active income. This gives you the option to quit your job and do something else with your time. At this point, most people decide to set up another source of passive income which further leverages their time.

Done in this way, passive income brings the power of compounding into effect since one stream builds another and so on. What I mean is that let's say you set aside $30,000 for trading options, after a lot of preparation and practice. Let's assume you generate $15,000 on this money after taxes. After five years of such returns, assuming you reinvested all your cash, you'll have enough for a down payment for a house or a real estate deal.

29. When Is Forex Market Open?

When trading, one currency is exchanged with another, for instance, when you exchange the Dollars with the Euros, you say you are trading Dollars for Euros. The earning comes in when the money you traded with fluctuates in value over time. The rule is always, buy when it is low, and sell when it is high. However, it is not easy to determine how low is low and how high is high; to determine the low and high therefore one needs know the factors influencing the rate of the currency in order to predict the rate of the currency in the future. The difference between the rate of selling and that of buying a currency is known as the "spread" and it is expressed in "pips." A Pip is the smallest unit of any currency.

It is not easy to predict a market trend, and therefore are methods used to guide the prediction. These methods are the technical analysis and fundamental analysis. The fundamental analysis consists of policies put forth by a country that affects the currency. The central bank of each nation has a responsibility for the well-being of a nation, and therefore, it analyses the factors that affect the economy and make policies that improve the status of the economy. It is therefore important to look at the adjustment in the policy of the country of the currency you want to trade with and regular announcement because they are the economic indicators that bring about changes in the FOREX market. The indicators include interest rates, the GDP, consumer price index, and industrial production, among others

The technical analysis concentrates on market trends, trying to see if the current trend of the currency can reverse, and if it does, how the market will respond to the changes in the future. It looks at the history of the price of currencies and volumes traded, through reading and interpreting graphs. Mathematical tools used in making technical analysis include gaps and trends, waves, and number theory. The technical analysis uses three basic assumptions: history repeats itself, prices move in trends and market discounts everything.

For one to have a reasonable profit from the FOREX trading it is good to have a good risk management plan. However, the management should be based on capital preservation; remember that you cannot trade without funds in your account. Making big profits is not bad, but it is good to have a calculated risk. It is better to have a little success rate than to risk much and lose it all.

An investor should also have a trading plan to make sure that he or she achieves the set goals. The plan should not just be written down, it should be followed just the way you plan to buy household items; always buy when the prices are low and when your prediction about the rising of prices has a higher chance of being true. And sell when your prediction that the price might fall as a high probability that it will happen. There is no proper action to FOREX trading; it is having a good plan that is based on good analysis.

30. The Right Trading Mindset

On the off chance that you feel that your trading outlook needs a push, pursue these top tips sketched out underneath to figure out how to endure the trading game.

1. Observe the Actions of Other Successful Traders

Probably the most ideal approaches to get familiar with an aptitude is by watching the activities of individuals who have officially aced the expertise. Trading is the same as some other aptitude, and duplicating the procedure and work routine of other effective brokers can make wonders for your trading mentality.

Finding a good example among fruitful merchants may be troublesome, best case scenario, yet luckily, there are many fantastic manuscript that you can pick to get a knowledge into the mentality of those dealers.

2. Don't Let Losses Get Out of Control

A typical mix-up among tenderfoots in the market is the manner in which they deal with their losing exchanges. For the most part, fledgling merchants sit tight for a losing exchange to wind up gainful once more, as they would prefer not to close the exchange misfortune. As should be obvious, feelings are again meddling with objective trading choices which can be in all respects exorbitant over the long haul.

In the event that you lose half of your trading account, you will need to make a 100% come back to be equal the initial investment! This can be an exceptionally extreme endeavor.

Rather, attempt to oversee losing positions like an expert dealer, who are eager with failures. On the off chance that one of their exchanges is marginally in short, flagging that their exchange arrangement is not happening true to form, effective brokers will close that exchange and proceed onward. They cut their failures off, and let their champs run. Over the long haul, this can have a genuine effect to your primary concern.

3. Remind Yourself that the Market Does not Owe You Anything

One regular misstep that numerous dealers persistently make is over trading the market. Particularly after an exchange turns out badly, a few dealers want to pursue the market for exchange openings, just to amass strong misfortunes before the day's over.

This is not the means by which the market works. The market does not owe you anything, and it may be a savvy choice to rehash this mantra each morning you wake up. Some days there are incredibly rewarding exchange arrangements, and the different days there may be nothing.

This point firmly identifies with the past purpose of controlling your feelings and having trading discipline. Try not to feel irate at the market once an exchange transforms into a washout – recollect, the market has no feelings about you by any stretch of the imagination.

4. Keep Learning

Training is likely one of the most significant elements that different effective merchants from fruitless ones.

Regardless of whether you as of now have the correct attitude, you need a strong establishment of the business sectors to comprehend the purposes for certain value moves or market responses. While there are numerous ideas in trading worth learning, your most solid option is continue learning until you discover the instruments that best suit your needs and trading style.

Attempt to go through at any rate one hour before sleep time to peruse a trading manuscript so as to get a knowledge into the acts of other effective dealers. What's more, web based trading courses are likewise an extraordinary method to expand your insight about the business sectors.

5. Keep a Trading Journal and Make Regular Retrospectives

Another incredible method to accomplish an effective merchant's mentality is by keeping a trading diary. Trading diaries are much the same as customary journals – just that they incorporate the exchanges you make. Diaries comprise of diary passages, which can cover whatever you contemplate a specific exchange.

When you close your exchange, build up the propensity to refresh its diary section. Standard diary passages incorporate the money pair that you exchange, the reasons why you got into an exchange, its entrance and leave levels, and extra market analyses. When you close your exchange, build up the propensity to refresh its diary passage by the exchange's benefit or misfortune, and any extra remarks which may give a knowledge into the exhibition of the exchange.

Causing standard diary checks to can uncover an abundance of data about your regular trading designs that lead to losing exchanges. Perhaps most of your pullback exchanges transformed into washouts? Your trading diary will demonstrate that and help you to improve your trading aptitudes.

6. Get in the Right Trader's Mindset

Brokers can profit a ton from moving toward the market from a quiet and loosened up attitude. In the event that you have legitimate risk the board rules set up, there is no compelling reason to stress over exchanges by any means. At last, what can turn out badly?

Regardless of whether an exchange hits your stop-misfortune level, it's not the part of the arrangement. Losing exchanges happen constantly, and even proficient brokers have a triumphant rate nearer to half than you may might suspect. With a sufficiently high reward-to-risk proportion, which is the proportion of your potential benefit and potential misfortune on a solitary exchange, regardless you will wind up in benefit even with a half winning rate.

A losing exchange does not mean anything individual. Markets go all over constantly, and you need confidence in your market examination. Keep in mind, markets don't have feelings, and dealers who abstain from surrendering to their very own feelings will in general fundamentally outflank merchants who let their feelings meddle with their trading choices.

Having a morning schedule may likewise assist a ton with approaching trading loose. Have a go at getting up sooner than expected, work out or think and sit before your trading work area with confidence in your examination and risk the executive's standards.

7. Control Your Emotions

Feelings assume a major job in trading. In a perfect world, there would be no feelings connected to the business sectors and all dealers would break down exchange arrangements from a totally target angle. In any case, most of merchants are still people with feelings, for example, dread and insatiability, which as a rule meddle with an objective basic leadership process.

Unavoidably, there is dread engaged with a losing position and eagerness when a position turns green. Our activity as merchants is to figure out how to control those feelings so we can keep up a reasonable image of the market and settle on normal trading choices.

31. Day Trading

Day trading is a great option to gain your financial freedom in a short time.

If you're brand-new to trading, keep reading since this guide to describe precisely what the day of trading is.

Day trading is a wild, exciting, and often exhausting business. When you should be a day trader, so you need to be willing to make fast choices.

You need likewise to make sure when dealing since there will be absolutely nothing rewarding to purchase for some days, and it will appear to others that whatever is losing cash, and being is a crucial ability.

You may desire to discover a part-time trading position if you're looking to make additional money without devoting to trading complete time. Now, this doesn't mean you should go-go trading when you don't have much else to do, and it's always necessary to insist on taking 100 per cent Effort any time you purchase, even though you don't have the faith you'll lose cash at the end of the day.

How Day Trading Works

How does Day Trading work? As Robert Deel keeps in mind, the meaning of a day trader is somebody who goes into the marketplace eventually throughout the day and is completely in money by the end of the day. At no time does a day trader bring a position overnight.

It is needed for you to select the ideal timing of entering into and bailing out of the stock for taking advantage of short-term investing. This is how all the procedure works.

Prior to beginning share investing through online financial investment companies, you ought to collect concrete info on the variety of dissatisfied and pleased client of the business. Such details are quickly readily available for the consumer to utilize any share brokerage company. The company without such info or declining to offer them ought to be prevented as they may posture severe danger in the future.

With the share financial investment being technologized, some companies declare for having actually made great amount through traders from the choices and pointers they supplied to them. Once again, you must choose to decline and having an extensive search to choose the info that these online trading companies offer to you.

You may want riding momentum of any stock and bail out prior to the twist in turn. Specialists feel that it is in some cases, much better for selecting blended methods while investing in brief term stocks.

For people who are searching for techniques while getting associated with such a design of share investing, they need to safeguard themselves from the possible negatives of the trading.

Day Trading generally includes considerable time financial investments, as day-to-day changes tend to show market beliefs instead of the real efficiency of the underlying stock. Day traders often count on chart patterns to time their relocation - one chart pattern that is frequently thought about extremely important is the bearish engulf, where an uptrend is totally swallowed up by a sag; this suggests a coming high drop-in rate.

The traders have lots of alternatives like the modern-day online trading or the traditional where one purchases and offers their shares being at the stock exchange. It must be kept in mind that modern-day approaches are far way ahead of the traditional methods as they work at a quick rate within the course of a day.

Traders are the 'quick amount' individuals, and they are typically having the affinity for getting swayed by the big talks of marketers and little brokers. Here, they can constantly get caught in a risk. A knowledgeable stockbroker constantly recommends preventing the claims of ads assuring fast and guaranteed gains through trading.

As a typical situation with all online and routine stockbroker dealerships, a financial investment company requires to have registration with the governing body of your location. As these types of companies are incredibly dangerous, the traders frequently lack wealth endurance and time required to make cash.

These stock financiers are needed to pay the companies with the ideas and time that their authorities supply. These brokerage companies start with their making procedure from the time you go into the company unimportant of the scenario of your financial investment.

Scalpers

This kind of day trader trades for portions of a point. This method is extremely emotionally requiring and has a high rate of failure. Prior to you choose to end up being a scalper, keep in mind the stats: 92 per cent of scalpers lose cash.

Traders in intraday trend This sort of day trader persists in a deal until the trend reverses. This could take anywhere from a couple of minutes to a number of hours, depending on the marketplace.

Day trading usually needs a significant amount of operating money. Generally, you will need a total of $50,000 to be able to cover the selling fees (brokerage fees, clearance costs, etc.).

Micro-trend traders

Micro-trend traders, unlike day traders, typically keep trading for 3 to 5 days. We seek to sell a portion of a larger plan, then use stops if the planned trend reverses tremendously to deter the merchant from a deal. Successful micro trend trading requires the entry to be made at a point where the pattern is solid, preferably when explosively begins.

Micro trend trading is normally less demanding than day trading. Micro trend trading likewise needs less capital in order to achieve success.

Position pattern trader

How to day trade like a position pattern trader? Position pattern traders try to ride patterns for at least 5days.

The quantity of capital needed for position pattern trading differs; usually, the minimum quantity required for success to be lower than that for micro trend trading and day trading.

What Are The Benefits

The two significant advantages of day trading are fast exit to losses and instant outcomes. Day trading forces a fast trade of a losing stock which keeps the shareholder from sitting it out to see if the stock increases. Moreover, instant outcomes can assist a trader in tightening their abilities and assisting them in ending up being a more effective trader.

Day trading is the procedure of purchasing a stock and offering it in the very same day. An individual is thought about a day trader when they finish four or more day trades in a five company day duration and has two unmet day trade calls in 90 days.

Day trading is seen by some as a fantastic ability that is the only method to play the stock video game. Day trading does use numerous advantages, and maybe it is the advantages that draw so lots of to the concept of day trading

Day trading can be helpful for some individuals and not so for others. The option depends on the trader. The threats and advantages must be thoroughly weighed and the choice made upon an informed understanding of day trading.

In addition to possibly huge earnings, day trading has numerous advantages for those unusual people who can handle their feelings and hold up against the intrinsic pressures:

Due to the reality that there are so numerous more sellers and purchasers utilizing Currency day trading than buying in the capital exchange would still be open to those willing to sell when the time arrives. They can always appreciate the fact that investing on a currency day is easier than selling in the stock exchange because of the huge amount it deals with every day.

With futures, that very same margin might manage you the capability to trade a much bigger notional worth.

Another fantastic advantage is being able to trade twenty-four hours a day, five days a week. Another thing that makes currency day trading so enticing is the reality that you just require to put up a portion of the capital needed when making a trade rather of the entire quantity upfront.

Regardless of the advantages, day traders need to handle a variety of mental and monetary dangers:

Capital Loss. Even if a bulk of trades pay, substantial up-front expenses such as hardware, software application, and preliminary news services should be paid prior to one can start trading. Continuous costs such as ECN charges (or commissions if the trader is not utilizing an ECN), interest, real-time news charges, monetary analysis and charting bundles, and interaction charges should be preserved.

Michael Sincere, day trader and author of "Start Day Trading Now," declares it is difficult to make cash when the market moves less than 100 points in either instruction from the day formerly. Too lots of traders are going after to a couple of chances, indicating that just those fast adequate to acknowledge a chance and act are most likely to make cash.

Mental Addiction. According to Ed Looney, executive director of the Council on Compulsive Gambling of New Jersey, day trading is "like fracture drug, and it's a lot more addictive than another sort of betting." Some psychologists recommend that bettors and day traders are comparable because they tend to be competitive and of above-average intelligence.

As an equity trader, have you ever been locked out of trading due to a day trading infraction? Or have you missed out on a chance due to brief selling constraints?

Missed out on chances can be pricey, so we will take a look at a few of the constraints in the United States for day trading money equity items and compare that today trading with futures.

In contrast, a futures trader does not have the very same brief sale constraints. You can take a brief position as quickly as a long position.

Self-reliance. Lots of day traders are self-employed, working on their own and answerable to nobody. They hold true business owners living by their wits and, ideally, profiting off their own choices.

Bliss. There are a couple of occasions that can match the psychological high that features a substantial revenue made exclusively by the efforts of a bachelor.

Status. Day traders inhabit a practically legendary status in specific neighborhoods, comparable in numerous methods to the famous "quick weapons" of the old West-- renowned outsiders living by their own guidelines and making their own method.

Minimum Account Size

A pattern day trader who performs four or more round turns in single security within a week is needed to preserve minimum equity of $25,000 in their brokerage account.

A futures trader is not needed to fulfil this minimum account size. As long as you preserve the minimum margin requirements for your positions, you can trade as often as you like at a size ideal to your trading requirements.

No Short Sale Restrictions

Another typical battle for equity day traders is that in order to short security, there should be shares readily available to trade. And there are numerous reasons shares might not be readily available.

You will discover that there are numerous advantages to currency day trading if you have the time and clients to discover as much as you can about utilizing the system. Make an effort to do your research study and discover whatever possible about the fundamentals of this type of trading and then browse for the system that works finest for your requirements.

It has a lot of advantages to use modern-day financier. One of the greatest advantages of currency day trading is the reality that you are not restricted to just trading shares you can likewise invest in currency, home and products. You have more range which offers you the chance to make more cash with your financial investments.

Minimum Tick

When a trader shorts a stock, they are needed to cost a minimum of a tick above last traded cost. This indicates in a down-trending market, an, and an equity trader might never ever get to take a brief position, hence losing on a market chance. Futures trader can be brief the market simply as quickly as being long.

32. Understanding the purchase of Options

Let's suppose that you're interested in buying shares in Acme Communications, and they are trading at $39 a share. To buy 100 shares, it would cost $3,900 plus brokerage/commission fees. For many people that is a lot of money to invest, and if you are a savvy investor, you might be more interested in purchasing options that you would be in laying out that much money per share. Keep in mind that our discussion below doesn't consider account brokerage commissions.

Suppose that instead you purchase an options contract and the price is $2.50. The premium is quoted on a per share basis, but an options contract is for 100 shares, so the total amount you will need to invest is 100 x $2.50 = $250.

Now suppose that you're bullish on the stock, and you settle on a strike price of $41. Let's say that on or before the expiration date the market price of Acme communications reaches $47.

Your gross profit per share is now $6. You've made $6 x 100 = $600. Subtracting the amount invested, not including commissions your profit is $600-$250 = $350. That's a return on investment of 140%.

If you had bought the shares, you could sell them at $47 a share for a profit of $800. While that is a bigger number in absolute terms, your return on investment would be about 21%.

Of course, depending on your financial situation, you aren't limited to purchasing one option contract. Remember that the stock was $39 a share, so if a person bought $3900 worth or 100 shares, they could have instead gone with 16 options contracts for $250 x 16 = $4,000. While the direct investor would have made their $800 profit, assuming that they sold when the price hit $47 a share, the options trader would have made $350 x 16 = $5,600 in profit (remember for both options – not considering commissions).

The downside is the risk that the stock price won't exceed the strike price. In that case, you're out the premium. If you had purchased 16 options contracts, then you'd be out the $4,000. The person who buys the stock won't be out nearly that much money. Let's say that the stock dropped to $37 a share. If they felt it would not be going anywhere anytime soon and they should sell at a loss, the person who bought the stocks would sell for $37 x 100 = $3700 and only be out $200 from their initial investment.

Using this example, you can see how investing in options contracts has a big upside in potential profits but also a bigger risk in losses. When you are talking about trading a single contract for 100 shares, the losses don't seem like a big deal, but you can see that going for more trades means that you're going to have to have a lot more awareness of the risks.

Of course, the options trader has one big advantage that the ordinary stock investor will never have, and that is the possibility of betting on the stock decreasing in value. Let's suppose that instead of dropping to $37 a share the stock dropped by $10 to $29 a share. So, 100 shares would be worth $2,900, and our investor friend would have lost $1,000 if they sell at that point.

Now let's say that instead of a call you invest in a put contract, the same scenario you buy 16 of them at $2.50, or $250 per contract. So, your total cost is again $4,000. This time say you have a strike price of $35. Your profit is $35-$29 = $6 per share.

This time you've made $9,600 ($6 per share, x 100 shares/contract x 16 contracts). With your initial investment, you've made a profit of $5,600 on the decline in stock price while your friend is nursing their losses. Again, you made a 140% ROI.

So, we see that buying options contracts can carry bigger risks while at the same time offering the potential for bigger rewards. In addition, they also offer the possibility of reaping the rewards when a stock drops in price, something that just isn't going to be possible with normal investing in stocks.

Conclusions

The first experience with options trading is a complete asset explicitly delivered for those that are thinking about trading options, yet have following to no critical information and expertise. If you are new to trading options, at that point, we would certainly prescribe that you read this early on segment completely before choosing whether it's the correct type of investment for you.

Options trading is a generally intricate subject, absolutely when contrasted with some of the types of investment, for example, buying stocks, and numerous individuals are put off by the general thought of getting included. The facts demonstrate that there is an excellent deal that tenderfoots need to find out about before really getting included and beginning to trade options, yet the time and exertion required can be exceptionally remunerating over the long haul.

Even though it's a muddled subject, it's not excessively hard to find out about the essential basics. When you have a comprehension of what options contracts are and the fundamental ideas of what is engaged with them, the more mind-boggling viewpoints will sound useful to you.

An option is a contract that permits (however doesn't require) an investor to purchase or sell a fundamental instrument like a security, ETF or even file at a foreordained price over a specific time frame. Buying and selling options are done on the options market, which trades contracts dependent on protections.

Notwithstanding, options are not a similar thing as stocks since they don't speak to possession in an organization. Also, even though futures use contracts only like options do, options are viewed as a lower risk because of the way that you can pull back (or leave) an options contract anytime. The price of the option (it's premium) is, in this manner, a level of the essential resource or security.

When buying or selling options, the trader and investors the privilege to practice that option anytime up until the termination date - so essentially buying or selling an opportunity doesn't mean you need to practice it at the purchase/sell point. In light of this system, options are viewed as subsidiary protections - which means their price is gotten from something different (for this situation, from the estimation of benefits like the market, protections, or other fundamental instruments). Therefore, options are frequently viewed as less risky than stocks (whenever utilized effectively).

In any case, for what reason would an investor use options? Buying options is wagering on stocks to go up, down or to support a trading position in the market.

The price at which you consent to purchase the hidden security utilizing the option is called the "strike price," and the charge you pay for buying that option contract is called the "top-notch." When deciding the strike price, you are wagering that the advantage (typically a stock) will go up or down in price. The price you are paying for that wager is exceptional, which is a level of the estimation of that benefit.

Buying stocks and clutching them with the end goal of making long haul additions is one of the more typical investment strategies. It's likewise an impeccably reasonable to way contribute, giving you have some thought regarding which stocks you ought to purchase or utilize an expedite that can offer you counsel and direction on such issues.

This methodology is known as a purchase and hold strategy and can enable you to build your riches over the long haul. However, it doesn't give a lot, if anything, in the method for transient increases. Nowadays, numerous investors are utilizing a progressively dynamic investment style to attempt to make increasingly quick returns.

On account of the scope of online brokers that empower investors to make exchanges on the stock trades with only a couple of snaps of their mouse, it's moderately clear for investors to be progressively dynamic on the off chance that they wish to. Numerous individuals trade online on either low maintenance or a full-time premise; buying and selling consistently to attempt to exploit shorter-term price variances and regularly clutching their buys for only half a month or days, or even only several hours.

There is a lot of money related instruments that can be effectively traded. Options, specifically, have demonstrated to be exceptionally well known among traders, and options trading is ending up increasingly normal. On this page, we have given some valuable data on what is associated with options trading and how it functions.

CPSIA information can be obtained
at www.ICGtesting.com
Printed in the USA
LVHW050934231020
669514LV00002B/218